THE
DNA
OF ACHIEVERS

THE DNA

OF ACHIEVERS

•———————•

10 Traits of
Highly Successful
Professionals

Mathew Knowles

I would like to dedicate my first book to my late parents, Helen and Matthew Knowles, for instilling within me a strong work ethic, an entrepreneurial spirit, and an awareness of the importance of giving back, not to mention a passion for life—all qualities I learned from their examples. Additionally, they taught me to be a risk taker by allowing me to be among the first African American students to attend desegregated schools in Alabama and at the University of Tennessee at Chattanooga. Those experiences made me a better man. I am forever grateful to my beloved mother and father for their unconditional love.

Next, I would like to thank my daughters, Solange and Beyoncé— first, for being kind and loving people; second, for being incredible mothers; and last but not least, for leaving their mark on the world as entertainers and entrepreneurs. They both clearly possess the DNA of achievers. I love them dearly.

Additionally, I dedicate this book to each and every student I have had the privilege of teaching and lecturing to at Texas Southern University and Fisk University. Not only have my students learned about the business of music and entrepreneurship, but I hope I've taught them about the traits inherent in individuals who are successful in the business of life, as well as becoming better at critical thinking.

CONTENTS

Foreword ix

Acknowledgments xi

Introduction xiii

CHAPTER 1   PASSION 1

CHAPTER 2   VISION.. 17

CHAPTER 3   WORK ETHIC... 35

CHAPTER 4   TEAM BUILDING.. 43

CHAPTER 5   PLANNING.. 67

CHAPTER 6   TALK-TO-DO RATIO...84

CHAPTER 7   RISK TAKING... 103

CHAPTER 8   LEARNING FROM FAILURE.........................118

CHAPTER 9   GIVING BACK 135

CHAPTER 10   THINKING OUTSIDE THE BOX.................151

FOREWORD
Tommy Mottola

This is how it all came about: I first met Mathew Knowles around 1996 when the girls in Destiny's Child were only about fourteen years old. As then chairman and chief executive officer of Sony Music Entertainment Worldwide, I was in a position to manage all the record companies under the Sony umbrella. Each company had its own A&R department, but I decided to create a super–A&R team that was outside the record labels. I would then use my team of professional talent-spotters to feed them all.

One of my top A&R reps in Houston was a woman by the name of Teresa LaBarbera Whites. She found Destiny's Child (not to mention Jessica Simpson at the same time). Shortly after that huge discovery, I was sitting with Mathew and the girls in my New York office on Madison Avenue.

My first impression of Mathew? He was a very nice man—and a typically protective father figure, which I thought was good for those innocent young girls. Granted, he had limited experience as a music manager at that point, but certainly he had me and my team at Sony to help guide him. And he was very cooperative from the point of view of things that needed to be done. But he was not afraid to stand up for himself.

Experience does not necessarily make one a good manager, after all. In my life before Sony, I had been a manager myself, for Hall & Oates. Still, I did not have a high regard for managers in general. Most of them were imbeciles who happened to be friends of the band. Mathew got in the door because he was a parent—but he was also a smart man, obviously. Whether he had music management experience or not, he knew right from wrong about what to do and what not to do, which is always good. He opened up to people around him with more experience, which reminded me of my whole learning curve as a manager.

I was like a sponge when getting into areas I didn't know about. I found Mathew very much like that too. He would always take direction well. The greatest thing about him is that he was very protective about his act and very persistent. Like any manager, he wanted to get the most he could for them.

I am aware of Mathew's reputation in the industry as a tough manager. But personally, I always found him to be gentlemanly and polite. I am sure that around other people, he might have been more pushy, but every good manager has to be pushy sometimes. I mean, when I started out as the manager of Hall & Oates in the 1970s and knew very little about the music business, I had a reputation as being the most obnoxious and pushy guy out there—and it was all true. So I understand when people get a reputation if they work as managers, because you always have to be looking out for more for your act. At the end of the day, the ax falls on you!

Look, the music business pulls at you in every way imaginable. The minute artists start to get some fame (or notoriety, as the case may be) and things begin to change on every level, they think, "Wow, I am getting it right, and this is all because of me." And then when they get more attention and finally make it over that line of going from notoriety to stardom—and then into global stardom and superstardom—lots of things happen inside their minds, such as "I am the boss of my own show," and "I know what I'm doing," and "I am going to call all of my own shots from now on."

So my advice to Mathew was simple: "Just tell Beyoncé to try to stay grounded. Keep it real. And always be open to suggestions." Most important, I added, "Please tell Beyoncé to remain humble and teachable all the time—that will keep her fresh and on her toes."

Trust me: the minute you think you have the winning formula, that's usually the moment when you lose it.

ACKNOWLEDGMENTS

Initially, I would like to acknowledge that a power greater than myself exists in the universe. Next, I would like to thank thirty of my friends and acquaintances—some from corporate America, some from the music industry, and some who are entrepreneurs—who took time out of their extremely busy schedules to be interviewed for this book. I've known most of them for quite some time, and I've both watched and learned from their successes as well as their occasional failures.

Thanks, also, to Chiquita Knowles Ash, my sister, who every day becomes a better friend to me; to Lin Almanza, my tireless assistant, who for fourteen years has worked endless hours to support me; to Johnnie Roberts, James Patrick Herman, and Cheryl Alexander for giving their time, energy, and expertise to make this book the very best it could be; to past and present members of my Music World Entertainment staff who have worked so hard to assist in all of our successes over the years; and to that special person in my life who loves me—unconditionally.

I extend my appreciation to all the people out there who suit up, show up, and work hard every day, giving it their very best and learning along the way. The most important lesson to learn? Don't ever be discouraged by negativity. Have the vision that one day, your passion will come to fruition. Remember: it starts with believing in yourself! I already believe in your potential, which is truly limitless. I acknowledge you and applaud your efforts to succeed in life.

And finally, thanks to Worth Davis, my first—and greatest—mentor. I now fully understand why you dragged me to all those boring meetings with old white men while I was at Xerox. They were merely the presidents of Shell, Exxon, Pennzoil, and Mobile Oil!

INTRODUCTION

I've been asked where I received the inspiration for this book. Throughout my travels—mostly on airplanes—I would occasionally start up a conversation with the passenger sitting next to me, or mostly the other way around. The number one question I am asked is "What do you do?" I'm always amazed at the incredible responses I've gotten from all walks of life—entrepreneurs, corporate executives, attorneys, and others. During one such flight, it hit me like a bolt of lightning: when I met those that were highly successful versus those who weren't, the thing they all had in common started with this tremendous passion for what they do, as well as a common approach for their extreme success. It was pretty consistent for most of them. Then I began thinking of people I know or have met one way or the other, and they also exemplified these same traits.

Throughout the book, I've included interviews with friends and acquaintances who have the DNA of achievers. I'd like to take a moment to introduce you to these impressive individuals before you read their own words in the chapters to come.

Chapter 1: Passion

Peter Castro was deputy managing editor of *People* from 2007 to 2014. Prior to joining *People,* he spent a year at sister publication *People en Español* as managing editor. He has edited cover stories on Britney Spears, Mary Kate and Ashley Olsen, Jennifer Lopez, and Jennifer Aniston, to name a few. Castro first joined *People* as a writer for the Chatter column in 1987. Three years later, he moved to Australia as one of the founding staffers of *Who Weekly*, *People's* Australian offshoot. In 2001, he was named assistant managing editor. In September of 2004, he edited the first Emmy editions of *People's* Hollywood Daily. Before *People*, Castro was a staff writer for *Vanity Fair*. He has provided pop-culture commentary on a variety of TV programs, including *Entertainment Tonight*, *Access Hollywood*, *Extra*, CNN's *Larry King Live*, *Good Morning America*, *Dateline*, *Today*, and *E!'s* red-carpet preshow, among others. A graduate of New York University, Castro resides in Manhattan. In 2004, he was named one of the most influential Hispanics in the United States by the Latino Coalition.

John P. Kellogg is assistant chair of the music business/management department at the Berklee College of Music in Boston, and an entertainment attorney. Licensed to practice in the states of New York and Ohio, he has represented recording artists Levert, the O'Jays, Eddie Levert Sr., LSG, Stat Quo of Shady/Aftermath Records, and G-Dep of Bad Boy Records. He also served as a member of the management team for the late R&B recording star Gerald Levert and represented him throughout his career. Kellogg is president-elect and a member of the board of directors of the Music and Entertainment Industry Educators Association, in addition to being a former board member of the Black Entertainment and Sports Lawyer's Association (BESLA) and a 2005 inductee into the BESLA Hall of Fame. He is the author of the book *Take Care of Your Music Business: The Legal and Business Aspects You Need to Know to Grow In the Music Business*, as well as numerous legal articles and editorials. A former vocalist with the group Cameo, Kellogg has been profiled in *Billboard*, *Ebony*, *Black Issues*, and *In the Black* magazines. He holds a juris doctor degree from Case Western Reserve University, where he also attended the Weatherhead School of Management. In addition, he holds a master of science degree in television and radio from the Newhouse School of Communications and a bachelor of arts degree in political science, both from Syracuse University.

Elsa Garcia was presented with a Lifetime Achievement Award for her years of dedication to Tejano music in 2012. The longtime Tejano singer is known as the first female producer in the genre of Tejano music and was the first Hispanic to have a Barbie doll made in her likeness in 1996. Her first huge hit was the song "Ya Te Vi" in 1993. Garcia, now retired, has had a successful career of eleven albums, four of which attained gold. The recipient of numerous awards, she was inducted into the Tejano Roots Hall of Fame in 2011.

Chapter 2: Vision

Roy Willis was the first African American graduate of the College of Arts and Sciences at the University of Virginia, the first African American student to live on campus, and a pioneer for racial equality. He fought for the ideal that "all men are created equal" and also successfully attended Harvard Business School during the civil rights era. Currently, Willis is executive vice president of Lennar Urban Development Group in Southern California, where he manages ten communities, including active projects in Los Angeles, Orange, and San Diego counties. Prior to this position, Willis was Lennar's vice president of operations in San Francisco, and before coming to Lennar, he worked as the deputy administrator for the Community Redevelopment Agency of the city of Los Angeles. Working with elected officials, Roy supervised numerous development projects in Hollywood, the downtown Los Angeles areas around the University of Southern California (USC), and from Crenshaw, Williamstown, and Watts to San Pedro. He also assisted city officials in planning and developing several Los Angeles icons, including the Walt Disney Concert Hall and Staples Center. Willis helped develop the 469-room Inter-Continental Hotel, 217-unit Museum Towers apartment project, and 372-unit Grand Promenade apartment complex. He earned a master of business administration degree in urban finance development from Harvard Business School and a bachelor of science degree in chemistry from the University of Virginia. He is currently active with the Los Angeles Chamber Building Industry Association, the Los Angeles Central City Association, and the Los Angeles Business Council, as well as a number of other civic and community organizations. He cofounded the Ross Minority Program in Real Estate Finance and Development at USC.

Jon Platt is an American music-publishing executive and a former DJ. He is president of North America for Warner/Chappell Music and spent seventeen years at EMI Music Publishing. Although he was born in Philadelphia, Platt considers Denver his hometown. He credits a conversation with Public Enemy's front man, Chuck D, as the main inspiration for wanting to be more than a local DJ. He decided to become a manager and relocated to Los Angeles, where he was introduced to Madukey Productions by a friend. He secured the crew a remix of 2Pac's single "Keep Ya Head Up" and brokered a publishing deal with EMI for both Madukey and producer Kiyamma Griffin, thereby establishing a relationship with Steve Prudhomme, a creative manager at EMI. In 1995, Prudhomme left EMI to join Warner Bros., and he suggested to his former employer that Platt should be hired as creative manager. It didn't take long until Platt made noise by acquiring the publishing rights to TLC's single "Waterfalls," one of the biggest crossover hits of the mid–1990s. He quickly climbed the corporate ladder, becoming creative director after one year and vice president a year later. He also successfully recruited Jay Z to EMI after the release of the classic debut album *Reasonable Doubt* in 1996. In 2012, Platt left his position as vice president at EMI for Warner/Chappell Music.

Dr. Ken McGill is an ordained minister and has been involved in counseling for more than twenty-five years. He holds a bachelor's degree in religion from Pacific Christian College (now Hope International University), a certificate of completion in the alcohol and drug studies/counseling program at the University of California at Los Angeles, and a master's degree in clinical psychology from Antioch University. His résumé of service includes a plethora of national institutes and organizations, where he specializes in counseling—individuals, couples, families, and groups—and providing psycho-educational training. McGill serves on a variety of boards that provide professional services to our society's most vulnerable citizens. He currently works as a private-practice clinician in Plano, Texas.

Chapter 3: Work Ethic

B. Smith is an American restaurateur, model, author, and television host. Raised in Scottdale, Pennsylvania, Smith attended Southmoreland High School. Her mother, Florence, was a maid, and her father, William, a steelworker. In the 1970s, Smith was the first black model to appear on the cover of *Mademoiselle* magazine. She owns two restaurants—the first of which opened in 1986—located on Restaurant Row in Manhattan and in Sag Harbor, Long Island. Smith's interest in décor and restaurant design led to the development of her first home collection, which debuted at Bed Bath & Beyond in the spring of 2001; she also launched a line of serving accessories in 2004. In the spring of 2007, Smith debuted her first furniture collection with the La-Z-Boy company Clayton Marcus. Smith has acted on both the stage and small screen. She hosted a half-hour television show, *B. Smith with Style*, which aired on weekdays on BTN and Bounce TV, featuring home decor and cooking segments. Since 1995, Smith has authored three books concentrating on recipes and presentation: *B. Smith's Entertaining and Cooking for Friends*, *B. Smith's Rituals and Celebrations*, and *B. Smith Cooks Southern Style*.

Deb Vangellow, a Ladies Professional Golf Association (LPGA) Master Professional, holds both a bachelor of arts and a master of science degree in health/physical education/coaching and educational leadership/psychology from the University of Northern Iowa (UNI) and Miami University in Ohio, respectively. A multisport athlete who was a scholarship recipient, captain, and letter winner in soccer and track, Deb chose to devote her career path to developing into a top golf educator. Her experiences reflect this endeavor. She coached Division I collegiate golf at UNI and led the American Junior Golf Team that traveled to Europe in 1996 as part of the International Sport for Understanding Program. She has worked with the Japanese corporate-sponsored "Superlady" project/Kathy Whitworth Golf Academy, Heritage School of Golf at Old Orchard Golf Club, Pine Forest Country Club, Camp Olympia Junior Golf Academy, and Sweetwater Country Club, all in Texas, as well as the Nike Junior Golf Camp at Pebble Beach, California. At Rice University in Texas, she teaches golf classes in the School of Health and Physical Education. Deb was the 2012 LPGA National Teacher of the Year and was recently inducted into the UNI Athletics Hall of Fame; the UNI School of Health, Physical Education, and Leisure Studies Hall of Excellence; and the Hall of Fame at Fairport High School in Rochester, New York. She writes for *Texas Links* and *Southern Gaming/Destinations* magazines, and she has contributed to most every golf magazine in publication. Her awards and recognitions are numerous. In addition to teaching men, women, senior golfers, and junior golfers of all skill levels individually and in groups at Riverbend Country Club in Houston, Texas, Deb is the first-ever national vice president for the LPGA Teaching and Club Professional Membership and a lead instructor in the LPGA Global Education Program. She is also a select invitee to the Proponent Group for the top golf instructors in the world and serves on many golf advisory boards and committees. Deb is a longtime and loyal Titleist/FootJoy staff member, appearing on the Golf Channel in two commercials.

Chapter 4: Team Building

Joe Campinell has served as president of L'Oréal USA Inc.'s Consumer Products Group and L'Oréal Retail since 1997. He joined L'Oréal USA in 1986 as vice president for marketing of the L'Oréal Hair Care Division. He served as the unit's senior vice president and general manager for ten years and took responsibility for the strategy and business direction of Softsheen (now Softsheen-Carson) in 1999. His twenty-eight-year career in the beauty industry began with numerous marketing and management positions at Colgate-Palmolive and Chesebrough-Pond's. He holds an undergraduate degree from the State University of New York at Plattsburgh and an master of business administration degree from Syracuse University.

Rick Smith is currently general manager of the Houston Texans of the National Football League (NFL). Smith played for the Boilermakers of Purdue University as a strong safety. He graduated from that institution and later served as a coach. After that stint, he coached for a month at Texas Christian University before going to the NFL. He became general manager of the Texans on June 5, 2006, succeeding Charley Casserly. According to the Texans website, he is responsible for all aspects of football operations, salary-cap management, and budgeting. He previously was with the Denver Broncos organization, first as a coach and then in the front office. Smith is an executive board member of Pro-Vision, a Houston charter school and nonprofit organization that provides educational, job training, and mentoring services to boys and girls ages ten through eighteen.

Candace Matthews is chief marketing officer for Amway and leads the company's global enterprise marketing strategy and global marketing team. Matthews joined Amway in 2007 after serving as president of Softsheen-Carson, part of the Consumer Products Division of L'Oréal USA, and vice president for New Product and Package Innovation and managing director for Non-Cola Brands with the Coca-Cola Company. In addition, she held senior marketing positions at the CIBA Vision Corporation; Bausch + Lomb, Oral Care Division; Procter & Gamble, Cosmetics and Fragrance Division; and General Mills, where she began her marketing career. Matthews is a member of the Executive Leadership Council and currently serves on the boards of numerous prestigious organizations. Her professional background and community service have landed her on the pages of *Ebony*, *Essence*, *Black Enterprise*, *Glamour*, *Salon Sense*, and the *Wall Street Journal*. *Black Enterprise* named her 2009 Corporate Executive of the Year, and *Advertising Age* counted Matthews among its 2011 Women to Watch. A native of New Brighton, Pennsylvania, Matthews received a bachelor of science degree in metallurgical engineering and administrative and management science from Carnegie Mellon University, and a master of business administration degree from the Stanford Graduate School of Business.

Neil Portnow is the current president of the National Academy of Recording Arts and Sciences (NARAS) and was formerly vice president of the West Coast division of Jive Records. After graduating from George Washington University in 1971, he started out as a record producer and music supervisor. He worked with RCA Records as a staff producer, was vice president of A&R at Arista and EMI America, and served as senior vice president and then president at 20th Century Records. He started working with Jive in 1989, overseeing the expansion of their West Coast operation and making Jive a groundbreaking, successful label. Jive thrived under his leadership as he spearheaded the careers of some of the biggest acts of the late 1990s and early 2000s. In November 2002, Portnow became president of NARAS. On March 24, 2011, his contract as president of the academy was extended for four years.

Chapter 5: Planning

Ken Ehrlich is an American television producer and director. For more than twenty-five years, no individual has produced more music-related and nontraditional programming for television—as well as single and multiartist and concept specials for network, cable, syndication, and home-video programming—than Ehrlich. With hundreds of hours of highly acclaimed specials to his credit, including the annual Grammy

Awards, which he has produced since 1980, and a yearly slate of other award shows, Ehrlich's accomplishments are unmatched. He has been nominated for five Emmy Awards, is the recipient of one Golden Globe Award, and was presented with the Producer's Guild of America Visionary Award in 2007.

Gerard J. Inzerillo is chief executive officer of the *Forbes Travel Guide*, originator of the prestigious five-star rating system and the travel industry's most comprehensive source of ratings and reviews since 1958. From 2012 to 2014, he served as president and chief executive officer of IMG Artists (IMGA)—the global leader in artist management, performing arts, and events planning—managing the careers of more than five hundred artists as producer, agent, manager, and promoter for 25,000 musical performances and events annually. Jerry, as he is known by most in the business, is a visionary renowned for his trademark innovation and the extensive network of contacts in tourism, hospitality, entertainment, and business he's cultivated during his four decades as a manager and executive in the hospitality and entertainment industries. Before coming to IMGA, Inzerillo was president of Kerzner Entertainment Group (1991 to 2011), raising the visibility of the company and the profile of its properties in the Bahamas, Dubai, the Indian Ocean, Mexico, and Morocco. From 1991 to 1996, Inzerillo served as chief executive officer of Sun City, the unique South African resort complex built by Sol Kerzner. He has also long been involved in philanthropy, especially with respect to children, education, and HIV/AIDS.

Colin Cowie is a South African lifestyle guru and party planner to the stars, as well as a television personality and a writer. Born in Kitwe, Federation of Rhodesia and Nyasaland (now Zambia), and educated in South Africa, Cowie moved to the United States in 1985. He is an acclaimed interior designer with projects around the world, including the Mira Hong Kong. Cowie regularly appears on the *Today Show*, the *Oprah Winfrey Show*, and the *Ellen DeGeneres Show*. He was a contributing family member to the CBS *Early Show* for eight years, hosted the television series *Everyday Elegance*, and is currently host of the daily wedding-planning show *Get Married* on Lifetime TV, on which he shares his professional expertise with brides-to-be on fashion, decorating, and other wedding-related topics. Cowie has been profiled and quoted extensively in many periodicals, including the *New York Times, People, Architectural Digest, In Style, Town & Country, Us Weekly, Reader's Digest, USA Today, TV Guide*, the *Los Angeles Times, Modern Bride*, and the *Chicago Daily Herald*. He has written eight books, including five wedding books (*Colin Cowie Weddings, For the Bride, For the Groom, Extraordinary Weddings, Colin Cowie Wedding Chic*), two cookbooks for entertaining (*Effortless Elegance, Dinner After Dark*), a book on living with style (*Colin Cowie Chic*), and three books on design.

Chapter 6: Talk-to-Do Ratio

Attorney **Ricky Anderson** cofounded the Black Broadcasting Network (BBN) with Yusef Muhammad in 2008. A managing partner of the Houston-headquartered law firm Anderson & Smith PC since 1994, Anderson currently represents a number of talents, including comedian-actor Steve Harvey, comedian-actress Mo'Nique, four-time Grammy Award winner Yolanda Adams, actress Cassi Davis, actor Isaiah Washington, and Rickey Smiley of the nationally syndicated *Rickey Smiley Morning Show*, to name a few. In addition to network television, movies, feature films, and pay-per-view representation, Anderson is the creator and executive producer of the nationally syndicated weekly television show *Big City* and the current chief executive officer and president of Big City Enterprises Inc. Named Entertainment Attorney of the Year 2006–2007 by the National Bar Association, Anderson also received the National Bar Association Presidential Award in 2008. He is an adjunct professor lecturing in entertainment law, music-industry contracts, and trial preparation at Texas Southern University's Thurgood

Marshall School of Law, where he received his juris doctor degree and was admitted to the state bar in 1992. A 1979 graduate of Benton Harbor High School in Benton Harbor, Michigan, Anderson attended Prairie View A&M University, receiving his bachelor's degree in business administration in 1983.

David Saltz has been a notable executive producer for music and media for almost three decades. This includes television, radio, online, multimedia, and broadcast of specialty entertainment and world-renowned sporting events, including *The Beatles Anthology, ABC In-Concert, Elvis "Viva Las Vegas," Elvis Lives, Elvis by the Presleys, U2 Zoo TV, Live 8*, and Super Bowl halftime performances featuring Beyoncé, Tom Petty, Prince, the Rolling Stones, and Paul McCartney; *NFL Kickoff*; NBA playoffs and finals; the European Cup 2008; and the FIFA World Cup. In 2013, he produced *Power of Love: Quincy Jones and Sir Michael Caine's 80th Birthday Celebration*; in 2011, *A Very Gaga Thanksgiving*; and, notably, Beyoncé's 2010 *I Am … World Tour*.

Talent agent **Andrea Nelson Meigs** spent her early childhood in the Compton area of Los Angeles and attended a private Christian school before entering the public school system in the fifth grade. After graduating from high school in Palos Verdes, California, Meigs enrolled in Tufts University and graduated with a bachelor's degree in English and Spanish in 1990. She studied at Spelman College in Atlanta and the Universidad Autónoma de Madrid in Madrid, Spain, going on to earn her juris doctor degree in entertainment law from the Duke University School of Law in 1994. She was then hired to work with Congresswoman Maxine Waters in the Los Angeles district attorney's office. Meigs joined Creative Artists Agency (CAA) in 1996 as a mailroom clerk, from which she was promoted to motion-picture talent agent. She was then hired as a talent agent at International Creative Management (ICM). Throughout her career, Meigs has worked with major talent in the music, television, and film industries, including Christina Applegate, Halle Berry, Ellen

Burstyn, Beyoncé Knowles, Solange Knowles, Jon Voight, Mark Salling, Cristina Saralegui, and the multitalented power couple Mara Brock Akil and Salim Akil. Meigs is a member of the State of California Bar Association, the Los Angeles County Bar Association, and Delta Sigma Theta Sorority Inc.

Chapter 7: Risk Taking

Paxton K. Baker is the executive vice president and general manager of Centric (formerly BET Jazz), a BET and MTV network targeting African American and multicultural adults. Baker is also president of BET Event Productions. He has produced numerous television shows and home videos and released more than forty DVD and CD titles. In 2006, Baker was appointed chairman of the Viacom Marketing Council. In 2008, he cofounded the Viacom Programming Council, which is composed of senior programmers from BET networks, MTV networks, and Paramount Pictures. Baker is also a member of the Viacom Corporate Responsibility Council. In July 2006, he became a founding partner and minority owner of the Washington Nationals, a major-league baseball team. As the general manager of Centric, Baker has led programming initiatives that continue to win awards, including a local Emmy Award, a GLAAD Special Recognition Award for "fair and inclusive" programming, a NAMIC Award for the show *My Two Cents*, a NAMIC Vision Award for the series *Lens on Talent*, and multiple Telly Awards. He has also produced two Grammy nominated solo albums (BeBe Winans's *Live and Up Close* and *Cherch*). Baker was executive producer of the 2003 and 2004 Source Awards and is the executive producer of BET and Centric's *Soul Train Music Awards*, the second highest-rated special on the BET network for 2009 and 2010.

Don Jackson is the founder, chairman, and chief executive officer of forty-two-year-old Central City Productions Inc. (CCP), a national television production, sales, and syndication company based in Chicago. For four decades, CCP has specialized in the production, syndication, distribution, and advertising sales of black entertainment television programs, such as the *Stellar Gospel Music Awards*, the *Minority Business Report*, and the *Soul Train Music Awards*, just to mention a few. CCP has produced more than a thousand shows for broadcast television and is a recognized giant in the industry for launching the first-ever black Nielsen household ratings survey from which all black TV shows are measured today by the advertising industry. Jackson earned his bachelor of science degree in radio, TV, and film from Northwestern University.

Alex López Negrete cofounded Lopez Negrete Communications Inc. in 1985 and serves as its chief executive officer, president, and chief creative officer. Negrete represents clients in the retail, financial, food, arts, government, health care, packaged-goods, real estate, energy, and insurance industries. He was named the country's number-two financial agency in *Financial Marketing Services* magazine's 2001 list of the top ten agencies. The agency was also recognized as one of Houston's hundred fastest-growing businesses by the *Houston Business Journal*. Negrete serves as a director of Greater Houston Partnership, received the 2002 Hispanic Achievement Award in communications from *Hispanic* magazine, and is a member of the Houston Texans' Hispanic Advisory Board. Negrete serves on the board of trustees of the American Institute for Public Service and the United Way of the Texas Gulf Coast. He is a director of Houston Child Advocates and the Houston International Festival, and treasurer of the Association of Hispanic Advertising Agencies board of directors. He has received the honorary Chairman's Award from the Houston Hispanic Chamber of Commerce and the first Lifetime Achievement Award from the Houston Chapter of the Association of Women in Radio and Television, and he has been recognized by the Houston Independent School District as a role model. Negrete received his degree from the University of Houston.

Chapter 8: Learning from Failure

Troy Carter is an American music manager who is the founder, chairman, and chief executive officer of Atom Factory, a talent-management and full-service film and television production company. Born and raised in West Philadelphia, Pennsylvania, Carter began his career in the music industry working for companies like Overbrook Entertainment and Bad Boy Records, eventually cofounding his own management company, Erving Wonder. In 2007, he founded Coalition Media Group, and in 2010 its management division, Atom Factory. Since then, Carter has established the careers of numerous recording artists, most notably that of multi-platinum Grammy Award winning artist Lady Gaga. He's an investor in more than fifty start-ups, from Uber to Dropbox, and has elevated himself to a fixture in the tech scene as a liaison between Hollywood and Silicon Valley. He's acquired heady titles like Aspen Institute Henry Crown Fellow and UN Foundation Global Entrepreneurs Council member. He earned a reputation as a branding genius for his work with Gaga.

Larry Lorey received his bachelor of arts degree from Bowling Green State University. He later became a top sales executive for Xerox Corporation. In 1975, he assumed the position of regional sales manager for Xerox Medical Systems (XMS). At that time, he was accredited for one-third ($1.2 million) of the total profit of XMS, selling mammography equipment used in the early detection of breast cancer. In 1994, he became regional sales manager at ResMed corporation, responsible for all sales of sleep diagnostic and related equipment sold to home-health care companies in Florida and Puerto Rico for the treatment of sleep apnea. Lorey worked with manufacturers in establishing relationships to represent various products and services. In 2010, he introduced a new product in the medical market for early detection of sleep apnea, which increased revenue by 110 percent. Today, Lorey is vice president of business development at Physician Consulting Inc. in Coral Springs, Florida. A consulting company in the medical field, it partners with primary-care physicians, increasing revenue streams and improving patient outcomes. Lorey has hired and trained more than forty consultants nationwide to effectively work with physicians in accomplishing these goals.

Ariana Grinblat was born in Houston to Russian-born parents. For many years, the family moved between the United States and Russia. In 2000, Ariana signed a record deal with Sony Music Russia and began a successful singing career, during which her achievements included six Russian Grammys, three Song of the Year Awards, an MTV Europe Music Award nomination for Best Russian Act, and a platinum debut album selling more than 500,000 units. She managed to do all this while being a full-time high school student and graduating with honors. She is currently living in New York and working on her next album, as well as songwriting and producing talent locally and overseas. She is a partner in a Russian record label and opened her first restaurant, Ariana, in SoHo in 2014.

Chapter 9: Giving Back

Nancy Brown has been chief executive officer of the American Heart Association (AHA) since 2009. During her tenure as CEO, the AHA has become a global leader in the discovery and dissemination of heart-disease and stroke science. Notably, under Nancy's leadership, the AHA announced a bold new 2020 health-impact goal: to improve the cardiovascular health of all Americans by 20 percent while reducing deaths from cardiovascular diseases and stroke by 20 percent. Nancy's drive to set a brave long-term goal at a time when many other organizations were focused on short-term needs has provided a rallying point for the AHA's millions of volunteers, staff, and donors. Nancy has also led the organization to a number of significant advances in the time that she has served as its top staff executive.

Rev. Rudy Rasmus is a pastor, author, and global humanitarian known for his outreach efforts to the world's poorest citizens. Today, Rasmus copastors St. John's United Methodist Church, located on two campuses in Downtown and Northwest Houston, with his wife, Juanita. Beginning with nine members in 1992, in twenty-two years the congregation has grown to over nine thousand members. St. John's is one of the most culturally diverse congregations in the country. Rasmus was formerly a monthly contributor to Oprah Winfrey's *O Magazine* and is currently a featured faith-blogger in the *Houston Defender* and the *Houston Chronicle*'s online edition. He is a 2008 gospel music industry Stellar Award nominee for the music project *Touch*, and he is the author of three books. Rasmus can be heard weekly on his show *The Love Revolution with Pastor Rudy* on SiriusXM's Praise Channel.

Vicki Escarra has been chief executive officer of Opportunity International Inc. since September 2012. She has also served as president and chief executive officer of Feeding America (formerly America's Second Harvest) and chairman of the Atlanta Convention and Visitors Bureau Inc., and she was executive vice president of Delta Air Lines Inc. from 2001 to 2004. She began her career at Delta as a flight attendant and rose through human resources, in-flight services operations, reservation sales, marketing, and customer service. Escarra is a graduate of Georgia State University and has completed Columbia University's Executive Management Program and Harvard University's Executive Leadership Program.

Chapter 10: Thinking Outside the Box

Danny Socolof is founder and chief executive officer of the Marketing Entertainment Group of America (MEGA), a graduate of the Wharton School of Finance, and a classically trained trumpet player. Shortly after college, he became one of the youngest live concert promoters in the United States. After promoting stadium gigs and emerging artists in clubs, he was selected by the Who to represent them in their "first farewell tour" in 1982. Returning from that tour, Danny formed MEGA in New York City in 1984. Passionate about new music and its relationship to technology, he lives in the Northeast and personally onboards each new MEGA client.

Reggie Saunders is global marketing director at the Jordan division of Nike Inc. and is responsible for product-seeding high-profile celebrities, thus creating an organic buzz behind the latest releases. Saunders's job is to make sure you think wearing Jordans is cool by making sure that the people you think are cool are laced in Jays. From Drake to Kanye to Jay Z to Mark Wahlberg and Cedric the Entertainer, Saunders keeps them all laced with the latest kicks—oftentimes long before the public has access to the shoes.

Dr. John Rudley is the eleventh president of Texas Southern University (TSU), the third largest public historically black university in the nation located in the fourth largest metropolitan region in the country: Houston. Currently entering its eighty-fifth year, TSU was designated a "special purpose institution of higher education for urban programming" by the 63rd Texas Legislature in 1973. Prior to joining TSU, Dr. Rudley served as interim chancellor of the University of Houston system and interim president of the University of Houston. Dr. Rudley has held numerous leadership positions in higher education, including vice chancellor for business and finance at the Tennessee Board of Regents, the sixth largest system of postsecondary education in the nation. He also served with distinction at the highest level of education in the nation when he served as special assistant to Secretary of Education Lamar Alexander in responding to the requirements of the Chief Financial Officer Act of 1990. Dr. Rudley received his bachelor of business administration degree from the University of Toledo. He received his master of education degree in administration and supervision, and his doctor of education degree in administration, from TSU.

1

Passion

passion

noun

strong and barely controllable emotion

a state or outburst of strong emotion

an intense desire or enthusiasm for something

a thing arousing enthusiasm

Origin

Middle English: from Old French, from late Latin *passio* (chiefly a term in Christian theology), from Latin *pati* "suffer"

In my hometown of Gadsden, Alabama—once a center of riverboat trade and heavy industry on the banks of the Coosa River—it was considered a blessing to be on the payroll of Goodyear Tire & Rubber Co. The local plant, in operation since 1929, supplied passenger and truck tires to automobile companies worldwide. In 1970, when I was eighteen years old, I landed a coveted job there curing flaps.

A flap is the thin internal layer of a tire between the rim and the tube. Curing entailed placing chunks of rubber by hand into round molds inside massive 700-degree ovens in short intervals. Outside the plant, Gadsden's subtropical, Deep South humidity felt like the inside of a walk-in freezer compared with the curing oven heat.

One by one, I would remove the finished paper-thin flaps. My hands were under assault the whole time. Bubbling, popping, fiery melted rubber spat from the molds, burning my skin and creating an odor that drifted into my insides.

Beware of some blessings! I did not enjoy doing that work. I did not wake up in the morning saying, "I can't wait to go to Goodyear so I can cure those rubber flaps!" It was a job. It was not my passion.

Education, entrepreneurship, lecturing, and music may be my current passions, but back then, sales and marketing sparked my interest. I discovered this by chance when I was in the third grade. With a dollar I had earned from doing chores, I bought candy at the neighborhood convenience store. Then I resold it at my elementary school. It was easy and enjoyable. *Thrilling* may best describe the sensation I felt. So I continued to sell candy. Before long, as my business grew, so did my need for more and more product. In fact, I was buying so much of the sweet stuff that I asked the store owner, "If I buy five dollars of this candy, can I get a discount? Can I get it cheaper?"

Why I decided to sell candy in the first place is a mystery to me. But that was my first unofficial sales job. The Goodyear gig in later years would only reinforce my keenness for sales. My many hellacious days at the plant left the searing impression on me that I could only build a successful career on the foundation of a personal passion. But that I would eventually end up excelling at selling, of all things, Xerox copiers, microfiche printers, and state-of-the-art medical diagnostic equipment was well beyond my imagination.

My stint at Xerox, from 1978 to 1988, was a remarkably heady time in my life. For three out of four years during that period, I reigned as Xerox Medical Systems' top salesman worldwide. Talk about passion!

Today, more than forty years into my professional life, I am still selling—in the music business, in the classroom, and in front of hundreds with my lectures and thousands with educational modules. My fire for selling and marketing MRIs and neurosurgical equipment, which included jobs for Philips and Johnson & Johnson, eventually burned out, and I didn't want to work in Corporate America anymore. Though the products may have changed over the years, my sales and marketing passion has never died. On the contrary, the flames roared anew when I dove into the music industry. Marketing, selling, packaging, and branding artists is the new world order in entertainment. I found myself selling people. Selling ideas. Marketing concepts. Selling songs. My passion for sales and marketing fueled a level of success well beyond my imagination when Destiny's Child, under my management, became one of the most popular global acts of the new century.

Let me be clear: before fate propelled me into copiers, medical gear, co-owning a hair salon, and entertainment, I had no experience in any of those arenas. I am very fortunate that my passion for sales and marketing has carried me to soaring heights. Passion is the nucleus of the success achieved by a multitude of blessed people I have encountered, whatever their walk of life—parent, entertainer, cosmetics tycoon, CEO, educator, or historic civil rights leader. From my experience, I draw one conclusion: of the ten distinctive traits that successful people possess, only passion—however you define it—is a precursor to success.

What is passion? For me, it is something that I love doing. It can be work. It can be a relationship. Most of the time, it is foremost on my mind. Passion is fulfilling. Passion is something I must have in my life; it's as crucial as the air I breathe. Whatever it may be—and these days, it is teaching, motivating, and lecturing—I am eager to do it. I wake up wanting to do it. I go to sleep at night thinking about it. It is a way of being and a way of living. There are nights when I don't leave my office at Music World Entertainment until ten o'clock. Then I lie in bed thinking, *Man, I can't wait until tomorrow!* My eyes lie open with excitement! I'm so excited now that I feel myself chuckling! That's passion. Passion is just an ethos for me.

Pick your favorite dictionary, and you'll find an ample range of meaningful nuances for the word *passion*. The operative definition, however, boils down to intense emotion—for or against, positive or negative—regarding some activity, object, or concept. Opposite impulses can orbit passion: anger and affection; desire and revulsion; intimacy and distance.

Determination, though it has value, must not be mistaken for passion. Even as I detested my every minute at Goodyear, I was determined to succeed, curing the flaps as best I knew how and surviving day after day, secure in my gainful employment. But success resulting merely from determined effort, I firmly believe, is destined to be unfulfilling, if not fleeting—no joy, self-worth, pride, excitement, or compelling sense of accomplishment can result. These are qualities that, for me, only result from passion.

Above all, passion is individualized. It can be a multitude of things, depending on the person. For Oprah Winfrey, passion is essential fuel. "Passion is energy," the Queen of All Media once declared. "Feel the power that comes from focusing on what excites you." As motivational speaker Tony Robbins sees it, "Passion is the genesis of genius."

T. Worth Davis Jr., my first career mentor, clearly had a passion for developing people and relationships. When I first joined Xerox in 1978, I reported to the Houston branch located downtown at One Allen Center. With Worth as manager, it became Xerox's number-one branch in US sales. Soon enough, Worth coaxed me into reading the *Wall Street Journal* from front to back and distilling the paper for the most important news to pass on to him. Later, he began inviting me along to the board meetings of Xerox clients.

At first, I did not understand his purpose or intentions. After all, I was this black guy who was merely a trainee copier salesman. And here I was in board meetings with only white top executives—the presidents of Texaco and Shell, for example—in attendance. Worth had a drive for relationship building that was his passion. I learned from Worth how to nurture relationships. He taught me that.

Does passion trump intellect? Yes, according to Dr. Gary Hamel, a leading management expert who hypothesizes that human capabilities align in a pecking order. I agree, given the example of my parents, the source of my first lesson in the transcendent power of passion. They came of age and matured into adulthood during an era when black Americans—"negroes" or "coloreds" back then—faced despicable racial discrimination in the deepest heart of the South. Neither graduated high school. Both had menial jobs in Gadsden.

My dad, a kind and gentle man who earned twenty-five dollars a week as a truck driver, convinced his boss to let him keep the vehicle around the clock. He used it in a side business: razing dilapidated houses and salvaging copper, other metals, and usable parts from discarded appliances and run-down vehicles. He would then sell the cannibalized finds. On weekends, Dad worked as a security guard at Gadsden State Technical School. Meanwhile, like many "colored" women of the day, my mother was a maid in white homes, earning three dollars a day. On weekends, she and her girlfriends made quilts to sell. Every waking hour, my parents' primary passion was taking care of the family—me and my two siblings—and ensuring that our lives would be better than theirs. Through their humble examples, I garnered my first glimpses of entrepreneurship.

During my travels over the past ten years or so, I have been fortunate to sit in the front rows of planes—in first class, no less. It is little more than a microcosm of people from every conceivable background and walk of life who have succeeded by virtue of passion. My seatmates have included fashion designers, clergy, art dealers, business owners, corporate attorneys, basketball players, and presidents of corporations.

The professional pursuits may vary wildly, but each of my seatmates has earned success through a similarly high degree of passion behind his or her efforts. I needed only to ask, "What do you do?" Invariably, the answer went something like this: "I am passionate about what I do. I love what I do. I'm excited to be paid to do what I love." And their faces lit up. They exuded energy and excitement. Their body language told you they were passionate to the very core.

School is perhaps the most inherently fertile ground for discovering one's passion. And examples of passionate discovery certainly are not uncommon at Texas Southern University (TSU), one of the largest historically black educational institutions, which is located in my adopted hometown of Houston. There, I teach "The Recording Industry," "Entrepreneurship," "Entertainment Management," and "Artist Management." I love to teach because I see these kids engaged. I see their willingness to learn new things. I see their passion developing. I have the opportunity to be part of their developmental process. It brings me great joy. And you too deserve to have joy in your life, as well as professional success. Never forget that.

In 2007, I met with Peter Castro, then a twenty-year veteran of *People* who would soon become the magazine's deputy managing editor. Among Peter's many editing triumphs are cover stories on Britney Spears, Mary Kate and Ashley Olsen, Jennifer Lopez, and Jennifer Aniston. For a time it seemed that whenever I turned on the TV, I would see Peter's talking head spouting incisive show-business insight on *Entertainment Tonight*, *Access Hollywood*, *Extra*, *Good Morning America*, *Dateline*, or *Today*.

Peter's journalistic passion was immediately apparent to me in his skepticism of the idea I had come to pitch: putting Beyoncé on the cover of *People's* sister publication, *People en Español*, of which Peter was then managing editor. I wanted to break Beyoncé into the Hispanic market. What strategy could be more effective than enlisting the editor of the largest Spanish-language magazine to my cause?

Although Peter loved Beyoncé, his editorial judgment was not easily swayed. "But Mathew, she's not Hispanic," he replied.

I told him, "You know, I thought of that. I wouldn't be coming here and wasting your time if I didn't have a plan about how to get around that." As it happened, Beyoncé was about to record her first EP, *Irreemplazable*, featuring Spanish renditions and remixes of songs from her second studio album, *B'Day*, including the hit single "Irreplaceable." The EP also contained a Spanglish version of "Beautiful Liar," Beyoncé's duet with Latina superstar Shakira.

Peter could see that I was passionate about endearing Beyoncé to the massive Hispanic market. I had a strong sense that, like me, Peter believed that Hispanic youth—part of the general music-buying demographic sweet spot—would come to embrace a diverse range of music. The offspring of Spanish-speaking immigrants, though grounded in Hispanic culture, would be open to hip hop, R&B, and other American music genres.

Ultimately, Peter couldn't conceal his passion for wanting to help make that happen. And although not everyone applauded the decision, in March 2007 he made Beyoncé the first non-Hispanic celebrity to grace the cover of *People en Español*. On Peter's part, the decision required a lot of passion, a trait about which he writes with great eloquence and heart.

You have to have talent and a skill, of course. But passion is the lifeblood of a successful career. If you break down the percentage of your life that's spent at work, thinking about work, or being consumed by work, it's more than a third of most people's lives. To me, it's inconceivable to be a part of anything for that amount of time without being passionate about it. The alternative is complete misery and unhappiness. I cannot tell you how many people I know who tell me they hate their job. To me, that's almost as bad as hating one's marriage. Let's face it: a career is a marriage. You're married to it. And to be unhappy in your job in my view is equivalent to being unhappy in a marriage. And what do those two things have in common when you are unhappy in a marriage and you're unhappy in a job?

You lack passion.

Think about the NBA. A lot of kids in the NBA have equal skill sets. On paper, you can argue, many can dunk, shoot, and make free throws like Michael Jordan. But what made Michael Jordan the best player in NBA history is that he had a passion for the game that was almost inhuman. There was a roaring fire that burned within him to succeed. I don't really think it was about the money—it was about the love of what he did. And you've got to have that love when you're talking about coming into an office for eight, nine, or ten hours a day, five days a week, having two days off and coming back to that routine on Monday.

I try not to do anything at work without asking myself, "Do I really believe in this?" I have to care about the decision I'm making. I have to care about how I approach my job. As editor of People *magazine, I wake up living and breathing pop culture. I care about pop culture. I'm extremely curious. Curiosity is a huge part of passion. I really care about the lives of these people we cover and the stories they tell, whether it's a really silly mindless celebrity or a veteran of war who has an incredibly gripping story to tell to our readers, and shares something about his or her life that's going to really resonate. I care about those people, and I care about storytelling. And I'm very, very passionate about those two things. If I weren't, I wouldn't be successful at what I do.*

You should have an abundance of concern about what you are doing and why you're doing it. Fulfillment is a really big thing. I think the happiest people in the world are the people who really love what they do for a living. You either have passion for what you do or you don't. If you don't have the passion, then don't do the job. Find another career.

Take the obvious people—the late visionary Steve Jobs of Apple Inc.; Mark Zuckerberg, the Facebook cofounder; and Oprah, talk-show queen turned cable-network mogul. What do they have in common besides billions of dollars and fantastic brands? I really believe this: they would do what they do for free because they love it so much. And that's what passion is all about.

During the spring semester of 2013, I invited John Kellogg to guest lecture for one of my music classes at TSU. Though we had known each other for years through our work in the music industry, this was my first real chance to observe John in the classroom setting. From the perspective of an educator, I gained a whole new respect for him. It was very apparent to me in how he connected with my class and through his teaching style that passion drove and guided his love for both the music industry and education.

I think one of the components of success is passion. To me, one of the chief elements in experiencing a successful life is giving your all and loving what you do. Before I met Mathew, I had heard Destiny's Child on the radio. I was living in New York, and they were on the radio with Wyclef Jean to promote their hit single "No, No, No." They were very young, and I remember being really impressed with the quality of the work I heard. I hadn't seen them at that time to appreciate what beautiful young ladies they were, but very quickly after that, I began to hear their story. I also heard about Mathew and how he quit his successful job to devote his time to work with his daughter and her friends. It was just a very inspiring story to me.

In 2001, I met Mathew for the first time. I was on a book tour, and I was appearing at an event for NARAS (the Grammy organization) in Memphis, Tennessee, where the local chapter was hosting an urban conference. I was in a radio station doing an interview for my book when I happened to see him in another room through a glass partition. I held up my book, and I pointed to Mathew; then he pointed back at me, so I told him we had to get together. Later that evening, we appeared on a panel together at the conference, and that was the start of our friendship.

I was very impressed that he took the time to come to Memphis to appear on a NARAS panel, and that was when I became aware of Mathew's passion. In 2001, Destiny's Child were Grammy Award winning artists, and so it meant something to me that he would come out to the middle of the country for an event that had nothing to do with Destiny's Child. It was obvious that Mathew was passionate about educating people.

Over the years, we had other opportunities to serve on panels together, so we built a relationship that was based on events where we were serving our community in various ways. Most recently, since I've been at the Berklee College of Music, I've asked Mathew to appear on a couple of occasions. He was more than willing to come in even at his own expense, just to share with the students his experiences and offer inspiration. I really appreciated that. We agree that we are very fortunate to be in the positions we've been in over the years and to have had the experiences we've had as the businesspeople behind successful talent. Like many others, I've always believed that talent is to African Americans what oil is to Arabs—our greatest natural resource.

For some time, I have felt strongly that we need people to be able to manage the business of those talented individuals in our community. Mathew and I have that in common, and we've been fortunate to represent people at the top of the charts who have entrusted their careers to us. As a result of being in that unique position, I feel that we have even more of an obligation to first, share with young people that success is possible, and next, give them the benefit of our experience so that they're in a better position to represent others in the future. This passion for humanitarianism runs in my family. My grandfather was a Methodist preacher, my father was a politician and a councilman in Cleveland, Ohio, and my mother was a teacher, so a feeling for service and teaching runs rich in my veins.

When Mathew was at the NARAS event in Memphis living his passion, giving of his time and expertise, it came back to him and to Destiny's Child. You see, the folks who attend the NARAS events (and there are about fourteen chapters across the country) are the folks who vote for the Grammys. I believe in my heart that Mathew's passion during that early phase of their careers contributed to the success of Destiny's Child and to Beyoncé receiving so many Grammys. The girls were tremendously talented, no doubt, but I think that by coming back and sharing his enthusiasm with the community of NARAS members, Mathew endeared not only Destiny's Child and Beyoncé to those folks but himself as well. His acts of fervor have clearly impacted the level of success of his protégées—Destiny's Child, Beyoncé, Solange, the employees of Music World, his students, and the others who have been associated with him. The most important thing we can do in life is be passionate about our work.

In the entertainment industry, it seems that those who are the most successful are those who demonstrate zeal in their talent. They are the ones who experience longevity and who maintain the respect of their peers and the public. My client Eddie Levert of the O'Jays gives his all at every performance, to the point that he's soaking wet—as anyone who has ever seen him knows. It goes beyond his desire to be successful. It's just who he is at his very heart. His desire is to give to people and not just the audience.

I was representing Eddie as his attorney on a matter, and we were in downtown Cleveland, walking from my office to another law office for a meeting. He was stopped every ten or fifteen feet by people, and the graciousness and sincerity he showed to each and every one of them was amazing to me. He treated all of his fans like they were his best friends, and that demonstrated to me the reason why he has been able to have an enduring career and why everyone loves him as a person, not just as a talent. They love Levert's talent, but that's simply a reflection of his great passionate personality and spirit.

Then consider MC Hammer. Hammer unfortunately went through lots of financial problems—many of which were the direct result of him having too big a heart. He zealously tried to help everyone he could. As it turned out, his generosity led him to financial ruin for a time. Now, however, he seems to be gaining momentum again after all these years. I believe that he is destined for success simply because his focus has always been fervently on helping others.

Also, there's Gerald Levert, who started a record company and studio in Cleveland and signed many talented artists and groups. He employed forty or fifty people over the years, creating opportunities for people to make it in entertainment and understand the entertainment business—including me. All of it was a direct result of his deep desire to help others in his community. He lived in Cleveland his entire life. Though he enjoyed great success and could have lived anywhere in the world, he never moved. His desire was to stay and elevate the city of Cleveland.

Fulfilling my passion is definitely one of the reasons why I got back into education. I feel my calling now is to inspire as many students as I can, not only on campus at the Berklee College of Music but also through the online courses I teach, and wherever and whenever I can speak publicly. I want to inspire a younger generation to believe that they can make it in this business and teach them the right things to do to experience success.

What precipitated this shift in my consciousness, I truly believe, are some of my experiences with Mathew. A few years ago, I heard him teaching. Then recently, he invited me to speak to his students at TSU. I realized then that I had more to do. I believe that we must position ourselves to be role models at historically black institutions. We need to make more of an effort to develop programs (like Mathew is developing at TSU) where we can passionately educate not only the next scientists, engineers, and doctors but also the businesspeople who will manage and protect the rights of our emerging and existing talent.

Passion can keep you true to what you believe in with all your heart. Elsa Garcia's passion, for instance, helped propel her to global stardom as an icon of Tejano music. When discomfort with the limelight threatened to dim her career, the born introvert relied on passion to pull her through for the sake of adoring fans all over the world. Here, the Lifetime Achievement Award recipient reflects on her desire to define what became a groundbreaking sound in the music industry.

I don't know if passion is what drives everyone, but it makes you stay true to whatever you choose to do—whether you have a passion for a career, family, or life in general. There are all kinds of passion. In my professional life as a singer, passion is what drove me to become what I have become today. My music career took off quickly, and that was over thirty years ago. But when my husband and I first got married, I didn't even know that he had a band! When I found out, I said to myself, "Okay, I can handle this." Keep in mind that I am a very introverted person by nature—I would never have envisioned myself on a stage, much less the lead singer of a band. But I had no choice, and when you can't beat 'em, join 'em.

Here's how it all began: I was at a rehearsal for my husband's band when they were scheduled to perform at the University of Houston. The singer suddenly came down with laryngitis. My husband said, "I've heard you sing in the shower, Elsa. You have to save the day!" I didn't have any time to get nervous. Now I may be shy, but I'm also the type of person that when there is a problem, I handle it—I take care of it. So I went onstage and made it happen. A few days later, the band decided to vote me in as the new lead vocalist. There were no other local groups with a female singer, and the rest, I guess, is history.

We started out playing weddings and quinceañeras, *and people started asking for 45 rpm records of our songs—this was long before the invention of CDs—so we considered recording an album. Coincidentally, there was a new twenty-four-hour Tejano radio station in town. This is the perfect example of my belief that the universe helps us make our passion and our dreams come into fruition. We played our record for the owner of the station, and he liked my voice. He liked it so much that he asked me to be the new morning DJ.*

So after ten years of working at a bank, I took a risk and quit my job. Before long, I developed a loyal fan base and had the number-one talk show in the area. Little did I know that the program director of the number-one Mexican music station in all of Houston was listening—and he wanted to hire me! This was the top Spanish-language radio station in the entire city. Meanwhile, when I wasn't on the air, I was always making my own music; that was my true passion. In fact, by this time I had recorded my seventh album, and one of the songs on it, "Ya Te Vi," was my first bona fide hit.

My mother had a huge passion for music as well, and she passed that on to me. She was a pioneer—and my main inspiration—but she never accomplished the things that I have been able to accomplish professionally. I wanted to do it for her so she could almost live vicariously through my success and realize her own dreams on the scale that I have. But this was all unplanned. When I received a Lifetime Achievement Award at the Tejano Music Awards, I looked back on my career and thought, "I did that?" Although my band has toured all over the world, most of the time I was on autopilot.

Success in the music industry basically boils down to three things: You go into the studio to record an album. Then you have to promote it on the radio and, these days, on TV. Then you have to tour because unless you tour, you don't make money. And then you do it all over again. I didn't tour to support my first seven albums. Talk about perseverance and not giving up! I didn't have a hit until album number seven. But I never lost my passion, and that was my motivation. What does passion mean to me? It has to feel like this is your purpose in life—the reason you're on this planet.

It's your mission to develop your own God-given talent. Passion has to drive everything you do, every decision you make, and every action you take. If you have no passion, you have no drive, hence no desire to take a risk. There's nothing wrong with being a follower—but the difference between a follower and a leader is the courage to take a risk. A leader is just born with passion. Whether you're a singer or you're working in an office, you need to have a big drive to succeed, not to mention a strong work ethic. Passion will drive your talent, whatever it may be.

Also, in my case, it helped to have a good partner who respects and understands me. He gave me freedom. In Mexican culture, the men can be insecure and jealous. But my husband was behind me all the way. I don't like drama; maybe that's why I am not a big telenovela fan. In my head, passion is a positive thing, and I don't like to see it portrayed in a negative way. To say that Latin culture is much more passionate is a vast generalization. It's true that there is too much machismo and that can be interpreted as passion when it takes the form of a man manipulating a woman—or vice versa.

I've never been into the machismo kind of thing. In a relationship, it has to be 50-50; it cannot be 75-25. So if, for example, you're passionate about your marriage, you should try my formula for success. And for me as a mother, despite my love for music, my children always come first. They're my pride and joy, and my biggest treasure. Without my beautiful children ... it could have made for a miserable, lonely career. I can see why some artists end up using alcohol and drugs as an emotional crutch. Thank God I never needed anything like that to feel good on stage, because I was literally surrounded by my loving family. That doesn't mean it was easy to get up onstage and perform in front of thousands of strangers, especially toward the end.

Admittedly, I became very self-conscious. I had to remind myself how good the performance went yesterday, and once I got out that first note, it was over. But I am not perfect, and for a time, I did struggle with a social anxiety. I am not ashamed to say that I sought professional help. Like I said, stardom was never my goal, and I was not comfortable walking those long red carpets at events. It was hard on my husband too—sometimes he would have to push me out of the limo. This is not easy to explain, but when you have so much unexpected success, it's surreal. Reality starts to seem unbelievable. And every time you release a new album, the pressure to make a big hit happen again can become overwhelming. But at the end of the day, all you have left is the passion that you started out with in the beginning. That same passion to make another great album is ultimately what got me through the hard times.

My musical career is undoubtedly my biggest accomplishment in life. How many people can say, "I've performed in arenas all over the world"? Or "I was nominated for a Grammy"? Or "I have five consecutive gold albums"? I have accomplished so much more than I ever set out to accomplish thanks to my loyal fans. My favorite moments were when I could coax my mother to join me onstage, such as when we recorded our live album on Mother's Day. After all, my mom laid the foundation, and she propelled me to where I am today. When we were small children, she taught me and my siblings to sing in harmony.

It's funny—I never dreamed of becoming a singer when I was a little kid. But sixteen years later, it happened in my life. It's amazing that the Internet was just being introduced when I decided to announce my retirement. I love it when people upload their homemade videos of my old performances, because I get to enjoy my success all over again. When I was living it, I had blinders on. All I could think was: I've got to record, promote, perform, and then repeat that cycle again and again. We were literally on tour for twelve consecutive years with no break and no vacation. Today I have a fun reminiscing with my husband, and I feel so humble—and so blessed. And grateful that I never compromised my passion for music.

Quiz: Passion

1. What is your passion?

2. Why is that your passion?

3. Have you found your passion?

4. If your answer is no, what can you do to find your passion?

5. If your answer is no, what is stopping you from finding your passion?

6. What are you willing to give up to find your passion?

7. Have you ever awakened in the morning and said, "I don't want to do this today?"

8. If yes, what do you think made you feel that way?

—— 2 ——

Vision

vision

noun

the ability to plan the future with imagination or wisdom

verb

imagine

Origin

Middle English (denoting a supernatural apparition): via Old French from Latin *visio* (noun), from *videre* (verb) "to see"

To visitors at Music World Entertainment's headquarters in Houston, there's no doubt about what the hulking beveled-glass-and-wood furniture in a corner of my office is. Crammed with a gleaming array of Grammys, MTV Video Music Awards, Billboard Music Awards, Soul Train Awards, World Music Awards, BET Awards, American Music Awards, and NAACP Image Awards, it could be none other than my trophy case for the triumphs of Destiny's Child and Beyoncé, right? That's certainly true. But what may not be obvious to most people's eyes is what makes it profoundly different to me—the way I happen to see it.

Those objects on vivid display are not mere trophies but considerable proof that not only my own personal vision but those of my artist has paid off in the music business. Every time I look at that doggone display case, I realize exactly what we've achieved—and that's not even including all the gold, platinum, and multiplatinum records over the years. That vision inspired me to leave Corporate America to initially comanage the artists formerly known as Girls Tyme into a hit act. Longtime fans of Beyoncé may recall that Girls Tyme is the original incarnation of the female group that eventually morphed into Destiny's Child a decade or so later. Girls Tyme became the Dolls, which became Cliché, which became Something Fresh, which became Destiny, and eventually the name I gave to them was Destiny's Child. To this day I am amazed that no one ever asked why I named the group Destiny's Child. I will share more with you in my upcoming book, *The Autobiography of Destiny's Child:The True Story.*

That was a tough period; members changed in Girls Thyme, I lost my partner to lupus, and I received many rejections from the music industry. Back then, my vision was not exactly fully formed. It grew and developed as our immediate goals came within reach. Not until after Destiny's Child's sophomore album, *The Writing's on the Wall,* dropped in 1999 did I imagine the then quartet blossoming into the world's best-selling pop and R&B group. The plaque for reaching that particular plateau is one of my favorite additions to the trophy case. But from the start, I had an idea of how the group should look, sound, and be marketed. We would, of course, end up tweaking those elements to evolve with the times and the fashion trends. But the core of my vision—the drive to be one of the most successful music acts of all time—never cracked or faded.

What is vision, you might ask? In September of 1996, soon after I created our ever-evolving blueprint for modern-day music industry success, the *Harvard Business Review* published an article on "Building Your Company's Vision." Few sources speak on management practice and groundbreaking ideas with more authority than this Harvard University publication. Authors James C. Collins and Jerry I. Porras wrote, "Vision has become one of the most overused and least understood words in the language, conjuring up different images for different people: of deeply held values, outstanding achievement, societal bonds, exhilarating goals, motivating forces, or raisons d'etre."

Today, almost two decades later, their observation is no less true, if my experience with a vast array of successful people is any indication. Yet, as I've repeatedly observed around successful people, life-altering success doesn't appear to be achievable without an initial vision, however we as individuals define that term.

In my professional life, I like to keep definitions (and everything else) as simple as possible: vision is an idea that I must bring to life. A central building block of an original blueprint is the question, "What if?" Feedback can be useful and valuable in the process of honing a vision. I had an idea for transforming the faith-based music genre. Since launching in 2002, my company, Music World Gospel, has mushroomed into the world's largest independently—owned gospel label.

Visions come in all shapes and sizes, and not all of them need to be so grand. My family's experience with Headliners Hair Salon, for instance, illustrates the evolution of a vision. In the 1980s, when hairstyles were bigger than ever before, we had the brilliant idea to go into the salon business. My former wife Tina, an expert hairstylist, would manage the creative side of Headliners, leaving the business side for me to handle. Admittedly, as a man who had spent far more time in barbershops than beauty salons, I knew only one thing about the world of women's hairstyling: that agonizingly long appointments were the number-one complaint of most women.

From this flimsy knowledge was born our distinct vision: Headliners would stand for peerless customer service, a goal we would strive to realize by providing the most efficient appointments in all of Houston. We would be guided by that vision from opening day to the day that Tina gave the salon to one of her loyal staff members of ten-plus years, and Tina began to spend more time styling matching ensembles for the members of Destiny's Child than their hair.

Few satisfactions in life are more fulfilling than experiencing one's vision as it unfolds. Mind you, while we never wavered from the core of our vision, elements of it evolved over time, particularly how we adapted the operation to actually deliver on the vision of providing service both effectively and efficiently. We believed that our target clientele—upper-income customers—would willingly pay premium prices for five-star service.

Those who run truly great companies understand the difference between what things should never change and what aspects should be open to change along with the times—between what is genuinely sacred and what is not. This rare ability to balance and manage continuity and change simultaneously is closely linked to the ability to develop a unique vision. A well-conceived vision consists of two major components: a core ideology and an imagined future. The ideology is unchanging, while the envisioned future is what we aspire to become, to achieve, to create, and ultimately to adapt. After almost two decades of market leadership and domination, Headliners was nothing if not a great company. And our core ideology—peerless customer service—was unchanging. By those measures, our vision was well conceived.

Some visionaries, such as Roy Willis, are just born that way. Full disclosure: Roy became my father-in law-after I remarried in June of 2013. I consider myself blessed to have an in-law who happens to be not only an influential urban planner but also a civil rights pioneer.

Roy Willis's ancestry already suggested that he would live the life of a visionary. His grandmother was one of North Carolina's first black teachers, having graduated from Winston-Salem State University, which in 1925 became the first African American institution to offer degrees in elementary education. "The motto of her school was, 'Enter to Learn, Leave to Serve,'" recalls Roy, a native of North Carolina who grew up in Norfolk, Virginia. "That," he added, "became part of my fabric."

Roy's grandfather, a well-known Baptist minister who helped found a school, reinforced the activist's creed. "After you get your education," Roy told me, quoting his grandfather, "figure out how to uplift the community that you came from." Roy went on to play a major role in widening opportunity in America's great educational institutions for African Americans and others, Needless to say, he did his grandpa proud.

In ninth-grade civics class, we would talk about current events in the local newspaper. One story was the 1954–55 Supreme Court decision Brown v. Board of Education, which outlawed segregated education. Thurgood Marshall, the black lawyer who argued the case (and later became the first African American Supreme Court justice) had been successful in persuading the court to do the right thing. But I had been concerned about the issues of discrimination and segregation long before that case.

When I was twelve, my mother and I got on a bus in Norfolk, and the driver told us to sit in the back. At the time, I was going to a black school and hearing the whites had better this and better that in their schools. I didn't like that either, but I didn't let it make me bitter.

The news about Brown v. Board of Education sent a jolt of electricity through me. If Thurgood Marshall was able to do this in the schools, I thought, then maybe we could do it everywhere in the United States. That revolutionary case inspired a vision that perhaps we could end discrimination—this unfairness—once and for all in America. I had the notion that maybe I could do something like Thurgood Marshall had done.

The path I decided to take would be blocked, at least at first. In 1957, I graduated from Booker T. Washington High School as an honor student and looked forward to attending the College of William and Mary. Located in Williamsburg, about fifty miles from Norfolk, it was the second oldest college in the United States, behind Harvard. None other than Thomas Jefferson, draftsman of the Declaration of Independence and the third US president, was educated there. So were President James Monroe and US Supreme Court Chief Justice John Marshall. Nearby was Jamestown, where the first African slaves landed.

Sure I was attracted to the historic surroundings, but honestly, the most appealing aspect of William and Mary is that it fit my financial circumstances. I didn't have the necessary resources to go to college, but my physics teacher had encouraged me to apply. William and Mary, he told me, had a program funded by the federal government to help finance the studies of science and engineering students. The initiative was part of the broader space race between the United States and the Soviet Union. My teacher was confident that I would be accepted as well as land a work-study position to pay my way.

He was wrong: William and Mary informed me that I would not be accepted. But the decision caused a quite a public brouhaha. Black newspapers and white newspapers alike wrote stories about my surprising rejection. Everything happens for a reason, and there can ultimately be a positive outcome when bad things happen, although you might not see it for many years to come. My favorable results arrived rather quickly. Norfolk State University, a black school that had been following the news of my rejection, took me in. There, I became one of the top preengineering students. At the time, my chemistry teacher was working on a PhD at the University of Virginia, and he suggested that I try to transfer to UVA. After my second year at Norfolk, I took his advice, applied, and was admitted to the School of Engineering.

What I didn't know at the time was this: UVA would admit black students to the School of Engineering only because it was a curriculum not offered by black colleges. But I couldn't go to the College of Arts and Sciences, for example, because school administrators would say, "You can go to black colleges—Norfolk State or Virginia State." I believe that was the prevailing practice. I entered the engineering school in 1959 and quickly made the dean's list. My family being very much involved in civil rights, I said, "I want to transfer into the College of Arts and Sciences."

UVA had been founded by Thomas Jefferson as his solution for keeping Virginia's blue-blood men from going off to the Ivy League and returning with corrupted values. "Country club of the South," they used to call it. No blacks, no women. When UVA balked at my application, my reaction, in effect, was, "Would Jefferson agree?" Why couldn't I, an honor student, transfer? I reminded the UVA community of Jefferson's preamble to the Constitution, "All men are created equal ..." It was a historic moment—amid the turbulent backdrop of Freedom Riders and student sit-ins at segregated food counters—for Jefferson's fine university to put the author's words into practice. My admission would be the living example of his creed of equality. After some back and forth, I got a letter admitting me as the first African American to integrate the College of Arts and Sciences at the University of Virginia in January 1960.

Since my time there, UVA has significantly opened the door of opportunity for all. The number of UVA's African American alumni has grown to more than 10,000. The first women were admitted a decade after I entered, and a white women is, in fact, now president. When you go to UVA today, it looks like the United Nations. I felt great pride when the university, which awarded me a BS in chemistry in 1962, later honored me with a humanitarian award in 2009.

With my degree, I began a series of short-lived careers, first as a chemist for DuPont and then as an army lieutenant for two years. After leaving the army in 1965 and returning to the United States, I applied to Howard University Law School. Finally, I would begin following in Thurgood Marshall's footsteps. But when I first got to Howard in September 1965, I realized it wasn't quite what I thought.

Events were changing my notion about what was—and was not— possible. The Watts riots broke out within the start of class. The War on Poverty would be rolling out next. I saw that the court was not the only solution for dealing with discrimination. I dropped out and chose a new path: business. But there would be racial barriers to break down in that arena too.

I soon found a job with IBM. As I grew more and more interested in business, though, I decided to return to school to better equip myself for the business world. That led me to Harvard Business School, perhaps the most prestigious institution of business learning in the world. But the world that I discovered when I arrived shocked me: I was the only African American in my class back in 1967. As I recall, I was one of only three African Americans in the entire 1967 freshman class. (At the time, there were maybe a hundred black MBAs in the country.) And here I'd been under the impression that Harvard was so liberal and different from the University of Virginia.

To its credit, Harvard embraced the need for change—after a sometimes tense back and forth over an affirmative-action plan—and financed a recruitment push, with me as one of the ringleaders. On April 4, 1968, Martin Luther King Jr. was assassinated. Riots had spread to cities all around the country when we began recruiting trips to Howard University, Spellman, and other black institutions. The results were strong and swift: twenty-nine African Americans in the class behind mine and seventy-five the next year out. We helped recruit more than a hundred students in two years, as well as the first African American faculty members.

Soon, I began putting my Harvard MBA to use. My first attempt, launching a restaurant in Berkeley's East Bay within the predominantly black community, didn't work out. Management problems killed it. Next, I tried the urban-development field and parlayed my interests into a job under Willy Brown, San Francisco's first black mayor, to revitalize urban areas. The result: the Gardens, considered one of the leading mixed-use communities—arts, culture, and retail—in the United States.

In Los Angeles, I had the opportunity to serve Bill Bradley, the first black mayor there. He wanted to make LA into an international city, with tall buildings and cultural facilities in the downtown area, which was really blighted. For the next twelve years, I helped develop Walt Disney, office towers, and hotels.

After the Rodney King riots sparked in 1987, I was put in charge of planning redevelopment of the burned-out areas of Watts and South Central Los Angeles. Part of the approach was close by—the University of Southern California (USC), which is virtually in South Central. My pitch was simple: "You're surrounded by fires and destruction. The community is saying 'No justice, no peace' as a result of the Rodney King verdict. Why not use your institution to make things better?"

The USC Minority Real Estate Development Program was launched to train urban planners and real estate developers from the community. It coincided with political goals. Congresswoman Maxine Walters, for example, wanted to get the community involved on the profit-making side of the rebuild, not just white people from Orange County. It's been running for a couple of decades, recruiting students from all over the country now.

I didn't consider the idea of vision as driving my experiences, decisions, and actions at the time. People could see the impact that I was having and referred to Willis, the visionary. But for me back then, while I was in the middle of it all, I was focused on having courage. It was a very dangerous thing I was doing, pushing for desegregation. With my religious background, I just saw an opportunity at UVA and went for it, and it all worked out. At Harvard, I simply focused on opening up one of the great institutions because it was the right thing to do and would lead to a better place for society.

I don't know if that's visionary. Visionary to me is such a lofty term. My story is a political story—trying to do what I could to open up American society for my people and other distressed people, based on the simple concept that prayer changes things. I came from a family with a guiding value: do the right thing, and if you see a wrong, right it. I tried to build out things started by my parents, grandparents, and towering leaders like Thurgood Marshall, Martin Luther King Jr., and Rosa Parks.

As I look at my life now, I am able to see things that I did that people characterize as courageous and visionary. There's an old saying: "If you don't know where you are going, any road will take you there." I knew I wanted to make America a different place than the America I was born into. I am most happy with the forty-plus years when I actually practiced what I preach. I got an MBA and went back to the communities from where we came with uplift in mind.

Soon after the turn of the century, after two albums, Destiny's Child was well on its way toward being hailed as a barrier-breaking act for a new millennium. With that status came a lot of appearances on the industry-events circuit.

Entertainment recognizes its own with events like no other industry I know. For each of the many elements of talent that go into the creative process, there is an event to honor it. Songwriters alone have several major ones, including the Songwriters Hall of Fame Awards, BMI Awards, and ASCAP Awards.

It wasn't long before I noticed the face of EMI Music Publishing at the writer's events. Each time EMI was called to the winner's podium, Jon Platt bounded up to the stage from a front-row seat. As the world's largest music publisher, EMI controlled, represented, had under contract, or administered the publishing rights of millions of songs and songwriters and held a wide margin over the number-two at the time, Sony-ATV. So it's not surprising that the towering Platt—known as "Big Jon"—was a regular presence looking out from the stage across the audience of heavyweight talent and executives. EMI was called up to the winner's podium more than any of its rivals, especially in the R&B, hip hop, and often pop categories that African Americans dominated.

On the basis of his event celebrity, I started a dialog with Big Jon. Not only was he a rising executive at EMI, but he was one of the few African Americans in music publishing. Maybe once a month in the mid-2000s, he would come to Houston, and we'd sit and talk about the business and the digital era. As a result of the relationship we built, Beyoncé and Solange signed with EMI and now have followed Big Jon to Warner Chappell Publishing, where he is president for North America. Many other top talents—including Jay Z, Kanye West, Usher, Ludacris, and Drake—obviously found his conversation compelling too.

Big Jon was open to doing things a different way. We had that in common. One example was the matter of "splits," or the division of credit among music composer, lyricist, and melody maker. Urban is sexist. In most genres, credit goes to the lyricist, melody maker, and music composer. In urban, it's fifty-fifty lyricist and composer. No consideration is given to melody. Jon and I really talked about that, especially as it related to Beyoncé.

Often, there would be nobody in the studio except Beyoncé. Someone would do the music, and she would take it into the studio. She was producing the melody as well as her vocals. She created her own unique singing style—for example, the fast-singing style that you hear on the "No, No, No" mix with Wyclef Jean. You'll read more about it in chapter 10.

Producing involves more than just doing the music. Beyoncé was one of the first females to get coproducer credit. Big Jon and I kind of changed that in the industry. He had ideas that weren't industry standard. That's what being a visionary is all about.

For me, vision is like this: I believe what I believe. And I like what I like. And I'm committed to go for it once I get to that stage. Vision boils down to trust in yourself. That's usually where goals fall apart with most people.

I run across a great number of people with great ideas, but they don't trust in themselves enough to try the idea or to go down the path. By the way, a lot of times, people who do that, they fail a lot. But you have to fail to win. People are afraid to fail, so they don't do anything.

One other thing about failure and how it relates to vision: I—and probably most successful people—don't go into something dwelling on the possibility of failing. Otherwise, most of us wouldn't pursue anything. My attitude is, you fail, you fail. Some failures have led to great successes. I don't think anybody goes into something saying, "I'm probably going to fail in this, but I'm going to try it anyway." There are people who believe in something so strongly. But just because you believe in something doesn't mean you're going to be successful at it.

Still, vision is optimism and guiding your pursuits with confidence. My vision in music publishing didn't come to me right away. When I started at EMI in 1995, I was doing the job like any other music publisher—just signing established songwriters and existing hit songs. And it struck me one day that I didn't have to do it the same old way. There was no reason I should judge signings on the basis of hearing a song. Did it matter if an artist hadn't recorded yet for a record company or that none of a songwriter's efforts had ever been recorded?

This became my vision: all that would matter was what sounded like great music to me. My background was that I was a DJ in Colorado. I would just play a record that I believed in, whether my audience had heard it before or not. I've always had instincts musically, and now I could use that in my professional life hunting for writing talent.

My vision was that I should sign undiscovered talents and help them achieve a certain level of success. I shifted my vision in that direction. That's when things became really more successful for me: artistic discovery, new talent, songwriters who I truly believed in based on the music and the person. Then we worked together to achieve success.

I worked with a lot of songwriters and artists who now are global stars. Most were at the very beginning of their careers when I got involved with them. They simply showed raw talent for making great music that I enjoyed and I thought would touch the world.

Warren Campbell is a songwriter I signed. He had no songs at the time. But he went on to create the gospel female duo Mary Mary and produce records for Kanye West, Dru Hill, Alicia Keys, Jamie Fox, and Jennifer Hudson, to name a few. He just had a hell of a career.

When I signed Jay Z, it was during his first album, Reasonable Doubt. *It was doing really well. But it was just his first album. The thing about it is, a lot of star songwriters today weren't stars yesterday. But when I met them, I thought they could be stars. Does it happen? Not all the time. But always it's the music first for me. Jay Z had amazing music that I believed in.*

Usually it isn't possible to execute a vision alone. You have to get people to buy into it. It's easy to get people to buy in when you know what your vision is. Some people try to get others to buy into ideas that haven't been fleshed out. Then, when you go to get people to buy into it, they pick it apart. Your idea can end right there.

I have a strong grasp of my vision before I bring it to others. I never ask for anything to help me fulfill my vision. I say what I need. You may believe that asking for help and asserting what you need to fulfill your vision is the same. Well, it really isn't. To ask a question is to give a choice to say no.

When I tell you what I need, I'm not asking. I'm saying this is what I need to make my vision happen. I don't say, "Can I have x-y-z?" I say, "I need x-y-z." This approach works for me. I've never been told no, because I usually have my ducks lined up in row when I air my vision. So whatever question you have about my vision, 99 percent of the time, I'm going to have the answer. If there's a question that I don't have the answer for, it's a learning opportunity. I go try to find the answer, and it improves my vision.

Vision comes naturally. The ability to have or conceive a vision is natural. You can't teach someone vision. If you are teaching someone vision, that's your vision. The reverse is sometimes true: visionary people can spot another person's vision. You could say, "Well, I have an idea to do x-y-z," and someone with vision could help you get to the finish line.

A lot of the time the problem isn't a lack of vision. It goes back to the earlier point about the lack of a person's trust in himself or herself. That's especially true in the entertainment industry. A lot of people see the glass as half empty, not half full. I work in a world where people have ideas all day. But only 1 percent of them try to take the next step. The idea is just a fleeting moment.

In 2009, I bought back my company from Sanctuary Music. Destiny's Child was experiencing phenomenal success, and Beyoncé's success was growing quickly.

Personally and professionally, I was encountering the pressure of success as I never had before. Ken McGill was referred to me by a friend as someone who shared his own life stories and someone who brought successful men together—particularly men of color—to empower them on their journeys.

From Ken's personal story and strong example, I learned the power of vulnerability and the fact that within my vulnerability lay my own safety. He shared with us that around 2007–2008, he accepted a position in Dallas that required him to move there ahead of his wife, daughter, and son, who stayed behind in Hattiesburg to finish the school year. On their eventual trip to relocate to Dallas, there was a tragic car accident that resulted in the death of his daughter.

I can only imagine the sense of loss and responsibility Ken felt, both then and now. His determination to overcome that loss, move beyond it, and continue to impact the lives of his clients in a positive, empowering way demonstrates Ken's vision for his own life, the life of his family, and the success he can inspire other people to envision for themselves.

Being a visionary is definitely a trait of successful people. Sometimes it means believing in things other people don't believe in, or sometimes it means you work harder to achieve success than others.

I've known Mathew since July of 2009, and since then, he's likely formulated his opinion of me as a giving person by observing me professionally and personally. By profession, I am a counselor, so moving people to success is what I have been called to do for a living. It is my purpose. And then generally speaking, I have demonstrated devotion, respect, selflessness, and a desire to see other people succeed by working doggedly toward success myself.

I think that most people inherently have this quality, but most definitely it is a trait that can be honed and strengthened over time to move us even closer to our own success. When I look at my own life, I think of all the people who have given something to me to help me become the person I am simply because they saw something in me.

I grew up in Texas and did not even know my biological father's name until I was thirty-three years old—and now I'm in my fifties. I still have not met him. My father's absence in my life certainly impacted me in ways, and I felt pain and hurt, but at the same time, it also kind of put me on a path where I began looking for healthy male role models and men and women of color after whom I could model my life. I simply didn't accept that because I didn't know my father, I might not achieve success.

Perhaps because of my father's absence, I encountered people and experiences that I might not have otherwise. Though it would have been nice to have words of encouragement from my father, his absence allowed me to convert my own pain into a passion in my personal life, as well as in my professional life, to help other people overcome their own pain. I do what I do because I have a deep calling, a vision, and a conviction to be a psychological and spiritual wounded healer, as opposed to an unhealed wounder. I challenge men and women to embrace faith and cultivate love for themselves and in all their relationships. That may well be because I didn't have a father's presence.

Like many, I would say that my biggest influence has been my mom. She worked hard to provide for my two older sisters and me. We were raised in Texas during the 1960s. It was a challenging time for me—even as a six-, seven-, eight-year-old. As I have grown older and come to understand what racism is, I can appreciate my mom's vision, along with her commitment, hard work, and devotion to raise three black kids in Houston during that era. From my mother, I learned to always do my best work, to work through difficult circumstances, and to not give up. Though it was a hard time, she also made sure we had fun, healthy, positive experiences.

My mom used to take us camping—which we jokingly called a "death march." We visited various places in Texas and around the United States. We started in a tent, graduated to a trailer, and now she even has a motor home. It took sacrifice and love for her to facilitate those trips, and they are some of the most meaningful memories of my life. I value them so much that I have recreated those experiences with my wife and my son.

Having vision can also create a ripple effect. Initially, it moves folks toward success in the sense that people respond to clear and strong foresight. They want to be part of progress and positivity. For example, I first met Mathew in 2009 when he gave a gift associated with $100,000 to create scholarships for three African American patients to receive treatment. One of the recipients was a traumatized male who, as a result of the opportunity, was able to save his marriage and family and also start a grassroots organization in the Dallas-Fort Worth area.

This organization now meets twice a month, where approximately seventy men become better husbands, better fathers, and better employees, as well as leaders in their own right. Through Mathew's gift, many have benefited.

Sometimes we act blindly, and we don't get a chance to know the rest of the story. In this case, we have had the blessing to see the growth of the seed that was planted years ago.

It's true in my own life as well. I remember I worked in downtown

LA—Skid Row—for about fifteen years, counseling people who were homeless. Word got out on the street that if you need some help, go see McGill at this particular place. It was one of those things where I was emitting positivity that even now continues to come back to me. I was meeting people and connecting with them, and many times that led to people writing checks or connecting me with foundations where I could provide service to help other people.

So it seems from my experience that when you have a vision of success, you're going to attract people who are successful, and simultaneously, the successful individuals, whether they are monetarily rich or rich in spirit, want to turn around and help others as well. It's like a wildfire that keeps burning, a gift that keeps on giving.

Another personal example is meeting Dr. Monica Roach in 1987 when I was working as a counselor at Union Rescue Mission. She was working as an intern in her doctoral program, but she also provided counseling services for the same population of eighteen- to twenty-five-year-olds that I was working with—the gangbangers. At that time, I had a BA in religion and theology, and one day she predicted, "Ken, you need to go and get your master's degree in counseling."

Fast-forward five years. I'm still in Los Angeles, still working with the same groups, and it's during the LA riots. Though I didn't yet have my master's, I had gone to UCLA and finished up a one-year course of study in alcohol and drug counseling, and I was still looking at a master's program. I got a call from Monica, who said, "I'd like to come to the mission and give a six-week group intervention on anger management." Of course I agreed.

While we visited, I informed her that I was looking into a master's program at Antioch University, and she said, "I'm an alumnus of Antioch, and I'm establishing a full scholarship there. I would be more than happy to name you the first recipient." So I got a $25,000 full ride—books and tuition for the full term of the program. I earned my master's in clinical psychology. The only stipulation she put on my scholarship is that I had to promise to give back to the homeless population. I knew in advance that was part of the plan, so for me it was a win–win. I was able to receive an education and then turn around and give back to the population that I loved so much.

I know that as a result of Monica's vision for my life, I was put in a position to eventually go on to the doctoral program, and I was also given an audience with others who could provide services and funds for the homeless. As a result of working at Union Rescue Mission, we were able to grow the Bank of America Learning Center from six computer terminals when I started to more than fifty terminals. Now men and women in the mission's rehabilitative programs are able to create resumes, get more education, work on college projects, and reinstate their futures.

We were also able to establish the Union Rescue Mission Legal Clinic in conjunction with Pepperdine University for people who needed to resolve legal issues. Pepperdine provided the legal students, and we provided the clientele and the work space. There was a need, and we were able to meet that need.

One of the things that I'm most proud of is that I worked with a gentleman by the name of Jerry Butler, who was my clinical supervisor. Jerry had a vision to start a mental-health clinic. Before I left Union Rescue Mission to work with the university, we partnered with Pepperdine University's doctoral psychology program and were able to start a mental-health clinic. We had doctoral students who came, and they ran groups, they did evaluations, they provided counseling for the men and women who were there who needed mental-health services. The clinic was renamed the Jerry Butler Mental Health Clinic in 2001 when he died. How wonderful to be able to see his dream become a reality. The clinic is still in operation today—all as a result of Monica's gift of feeding the vision into me and others like me.

Certainly, being a visionary is a powerful force and an instrument of success.

Quiz: Vision

1. Do you consider yourself a visionary?

2. If you said yes, why?

3. If you said no, why?

4. When you think about the future, where do you see yourself?

5. What ideas have you had for change in the workplace, world, or family that you've not shared or were reluctant to share with anyone?

6. Why were you reluctant to share your vision?

7. Do you think your vision is realistic?

8. What do you need to see your vision come to fruition?

3

Work Ethic

work ethic

noun

the principle that hard work is intrinsically virtuous or worthy of reward

a belief in the moral benefit and importance of work and its inherent ability to strengthen character

Origin

The phrase was initially coined in 1904-1905 by Max Weber in his book *The Protestant Ethic and the Spirit of Capitalism.*

We earlier spoke of passion and what passion means to success. Now imagine that every morning you are excited about going to work, and every night you can't wait until the next morning. My concept of work ethic is that when you live a life of passion, you never work a day in your life. When you are impassioned, the result is that you love to work, to create, to maximize on ideas. Work ethic starts as a belief system, and you can't have a work ethic without passion. The two are intertwined; they coexist, and both are necessary for success.

I saw my parents work extremely hard. My father would wake at four or five in the morning, and after working three jobs, not return home until eight or nine at night. Even then, I remember my dad sitting in front of his CB radio after dinner because part of his work ethic was giving back. He would listen to the radio for any emergencies and be prepared at any time to go and offer assistance to those in our community who needed help.

My mom would already be up when I would wake at six to go to school. She would have my breakfast made, my clothes ironed and pressed, and my sack lunch ready for me to take. She would be picked up and taken to her job as a colored maid; she would work all day and then come home to clean and cook dinner at home. I can recall the growth and development I experienced in sports as a teen—particularly basketball. Even then, I understood that in order to improve as a player and be better than the others, I had to commit to practicing more. This ethic landed me several scholarships for college.

In Corporate America, at Xerox particularly, I observed my peers work diligently to learn the product and sales skills. I saw how their hard work paid off for them. Additionally, I closely scrutinized the many artists I've worked with in the music business. One thing that is inseparable from their success is their work ethic—their enthusiasm and willingness to grow, learn, and take risks. I've seen no group with a work ethic stronger than Destiny's Child. I've seen no work ethic stronger than Beyoncé's.

As for me, I am grateful and blessed that I am still intrinsically driven to do the things I do. I normally work seven days a week—reading e-mails, answering texts, attending meetings, teaching at Texas Southern University, getting on a plane, or writing this book. I can tell you that I only work in passion, and for me that has been a key to my success. I hope as you read this chapter that you are inspired to really look inside yourself and determine, first, if you have the passion, and second, if you have the work ethic.

When I was planning this book, I knew I wanted the content balanced between music, corporate, and entrepreneurship as well as diversity in race and gender. The question then became, how I could find an African American female who was the ultimate entrepreneur? The answer undoubtedly was B. Smith, who has epitomized the strong black businesswoman in her work with her husband, Dan Gasby. Everything she put her mind to became gold for her.

She made history as a fashion model, setting a standard of beauty well before its time. She mastered the art of the restaurateur. B. Smith became a successful interior designer with signature brands in recognized store chains globally. She designed tableware and service pieces for classic dining. She designed furniture for national name brands. She conquered both stage and television. And she is a published author. Her entrepreneurial career spans a lifetime. If there was ever a role model to exemplify the characteristic of work ethic, it is most certainly B. Smith.

Work ethic to success is like lust is to love. If you don't feel it, if it doesn't excite you, if it doesn't motivate you, then you aren't going to experience it very deeply. Lust is the fuel to the fire of love, and work ethic is the fuel to the fire of success. You have to want to work hard. Someone once told me something about work that I never forgot: the person who's in early and the person who leaves late are the people who will always be great.

A strong work ethic means you have to be able to outwork people. Just like no matter how good-looking you think you are, there's someone better looking. No matter how good you are in a business, some people just naturally have abilities that make your abilities look dim. The only way you can stay in the game is through your work ethic. And so you have to work it.

It has to become instinctual. Look at animal instinct. Animals only do two things: eat and try not to be eaten. The ones that last the longest are the ones that work the hardest at not being food. It's a biological necessity. If you're slow and you're on the savannah, and lions are chasing you, you're food.

Success in human life is much the same. It demands an instinctual work ethic—which is, you have to run as fast as you can, be as alert as you can, and always strive to be number one. There may be somebody out there who's better than you, so you must constantly hone your skills. You have to be a diesel, like one of those engines out in Union Station. You see them at night, and they're still running. They don't turn off, because it takes more time to turn them on than to turn them off and get them going. A strong work ethic is like that. Your thoughts and ideas don't stop.

You also have to understand how to handle failure. That is a huge part of work ethic. If you are a chef, and you cook one hundred meals, you may mess up five or six of them, if not more, before you find the best recipe. You have to be able to handle that and keep working on the recipe. That's where work ethic comes in.

Being a woman in business requires that you work steadfastly and not allow people to mess with you. And a lot of that is fallacies of what people have in their own heads about who, and how, and what you should be.

You may have to overcome those who have no dreams or never think big. Many people don't. You may hear, "You can't do that, you shouldn't try that, you shouldn't attempt that." People may discourage you because your success or work ethic reminds them of what they didn't achieve or even think about achieving. It's sort of like flying a plane through turbulence. You have to expect the bumps and rely on your own inner direction if you are going to fly above the clouds.

Greatness requires tremendous ambition and tenacity. It requires an inner drive and a commitment to hard work—a commitment to the ethic of success no matter the obstacles or the struggles.

Deb Vangellow came to the offices of Music World Entertainment with a mutual friend who was visiting with me about one of my next book projects, *Racism from the Eyes of a Child*. Deb and I discovered that we know many of the same people. She has enjoyed huge success in her career as a golf professional and has coached more than a few of my friends.

From Deb's demeanor, it was easy to see how she moved so easily among accomplished, successful people. She carried the elements of success

WORK ETHIC | 39

effortlessly because she had experienced them firsthand. In our brief meeting, as we chatted about a variety of subjects—from our common friends, to places we've travelled for work, to childhood experiences—one thing became clear to me: Deb Vangellow knew about hard work and the discipline it took to succeed. Deb Vangellow understood the work ethic.

We are what we repeatedly do. Excellence, therefore,
is not an act, but a habit.—Aristotle

Wikipedia.com defines work ethic as "a set of values on the moral virtues of hard work and diligence" and "a belief in moral benefit of work and its ability to enhance character." Thus, it is believed that your work ethic determines how successful you are. I truly believe this. Always have. Always will. With this being said, I can assure you that I have had some speed bumps along the way that have caused me to reflect and remember when I get off track.

It was six o'clock on a Sunday night. A very busy day on the golf lesson tee was coming to an end—especially busy for me, as I was playing catch-up after some business travel with the LPGA, my other labor of love. It was a particularly hectic day at my very popular golf facility in Houston, and a number of frustrating scenarios had been building all day. I optimistically did the best I could do to get through the day, apologizing for many of the frustrations that my students shared (club members who were definitely customers and also friends) and wondering how quickly I could get things back on track to deliver the customer service I strive for and implement to the best of my ability. Many of the challenges that arose that day were things I had no control over but felt great responsibility for nonetheless.

I entered the golf shop, which had closed for the night. I had not been in there all day and wanted to pick up my mail from the past week and check in with my group instruction calendar for the upcoming weeks. My frustration from the day quickly accelerated when I found my organized registration binder in disarray. I had no idea who was coming, when they were coming, if they were coming—for a variety of events I had set up for the next month. I snapped, showing uncharacteristic anger and lack of integrity. I located a binder with upcoming program registrations for another event and removed them, right into the trash. On camera. Before I angrily departed.

The next day, I was fired from a job that I loved, after a seventeen-year tenure without a blemish on my quality performance for all those years. No one wanted to hear why I did what I did, because I never had fit into the teamwork that existed in this hostile discriminatory environment. I showed no leadership in this incident and certainly did not take the high road. I instead matched bad behavior and did not have the discipline to keep my emotions under control. I also showed a complete lack of respect for the customers who had registered for another golf event. This behavior was not indicative of who I was and how I operated. It did not matter. One and done. And I was crushed. A learning experience, without a doubt.

I am an LPGA Master Professional who has been teaching and coaching golf for the last twenty-five-plus years. My career has nicely evolved from being a very good competitive multisport athlete during high school, college, and graduate school to being a top teacher in the USA, receiving numerous accolades along the way and the honor of being in a select group who have the privilege of "teaching the teachers" here in the United States and Korea. I also have been our first ever national vice president for the LPGA. I feel very fortunate to do what I do, and while many of the opportunities I received came along in a right-time, right-place kind of way, I feel strongly that my work ethic, learned and developed in my earlier years, helped me become the person I am, personally and professionally. It really is a combination of perseverance and persistence. I definitely am a "work in progress," making many mistakes along the way, as described above. Given that the wonderful game of golf parallels life in so many ways, it is easy to share some things I value regarding work ethic. How you do anything is how you do everything. Both work and life, to me, have similar traits for success under this umbrella we call work ethic.

It is obvious in sports that a strong work ethic is required. A lack thereof will separate the good from the great. However, I was a good athlete all the way through to now, but not a great athlete. I can tell you this: no one worked harder and enjoyed the journey more than me. It was not a negative thought but rather a motivating thought for me to believe that I had to work twice as hard to be half as good. Which I did. It paid off in many ways (some very good performances, Hall of Fame induction at the high school and college levels, etc.) but the work ethic I learned and exhibited was more about self-satisfaction over a quality job well done. Nothing feels better than that.

As a youngster, I had numerous responsibilities at home that were clearly going to be taken care of before any of "this sports stuff" could even happen. I was thus challenged to have terrific efficiency and attention to detail with every task I did so that I could manage my time and do what I loved to do most. My parents were not particularly interested in my love of sport and pursuing this as a career. My motivation was to not only work hard to play the best I could but to obtain a college sports scholarship. I did both without a lot of support, much to my parents' surprise. And I couldn't be happier. Intention and attention.

It was an honor to be in a variety of leadership roles during my high school, college, and grad school years, including class president, captain of my athletic teams, resident director, sports program director, and the like. My work ethic in each of these roles continued to develop and flourish. The significant skills of adaptability, dependability, variability, and perhaps most important, relationship building have definitely crossed over into my career. No one gets anywhere without help along the way. Wonderful mentors have been there for me, and I am paying it forward with others as was done for me.

In the fall of 1981, I was involved in a horrific van crash with my college athletic team. One of my teammates was killed and others were seriously injured, including me. Thankfully, I ended up okay in the end, albeit with some bad visible facial scarring. Why am I sharing this in an essay on work ethic? I will tell you this: when your body goes through something like that, you are forced to start over in many ways—physically and emotionally. I am filled with gratitude to all who supported me during that traumatic time and believe my positive attitude helped me heal and get back to the optimal motivated team player I strive to be, even today. It was that accident that helped me prioritize and appreciate differently.

I am a continuous learner who now, more than ever, understands the value of a strong work ethic. I have learned, difficult as it is, the power of forgiveness and to value others. No one really cares about how much you know until they know how much you care. I have missed a lot of putts and have made a lot of bad shots. I put these behind me and move forward. What can I do better today? My work ethic will give me the strength. Process improvement because it is a journey, not a destination.

Your work is going to fill a large part of your life, and the only way to be truly satisfied is to do what you believe is great work. And the only way to do great work is to love what you do.—Steve Jobs

Quiz: Work Ethic

1. Define *work ethic*. Write it down.

2. As it relates to work, do you see yourself as dependable and responsible? If yes, why?

3. Currently, how many hours per week do you work?

4. Do you complete tasks or find it hard to focus on a task? Write your answer down.

5. Do you work well with others, or do you prefer to work alone?

6. Define *work integrity*. Write it down.

7. Do you go to bed thinking about work tomorrow?

4

Team Building

team

noun

a group of players forming one side in a competitive game or sport

two or more people working together

used before another word to form the name of a real or notional group that supports or favors the person or thing indicated

Origin

Old English *te͞am*, "team of draught animals," of Germanic origin; related to German *zaum* "bridle," also to teem and tow, from an Indo-European root shared by Latin *ducere* "to lead"

B ecause of my lifelong love of sports, I have studied the inner workings of team dynamics since I was a kid in the 1950s. But I was not merely a spectator; as an athlete, I played on the basketball teams of the University of Tennessee at Chattanooga and Fisk University in the early 1970s. Later, as a businessman who has always believed in the importance of empowering women, I became an early supporter of the Women's National Basketball Association. I decided to invest in the Chicago Sky franchise as one of the team's minority shareholders along with Destiny's Child member (and Chicago native) Michelle Williams.

For two decades as a talent manager, I have juggled more teams than I can count—sales teams, artist teams, label teams, marketing teams, A&R teams, street teams, production teams, merchandise teams, promotion teams, executive teams, creative teams. It would seem that only the world of professional sports involves more teams than the music industry.

At Xerox, scene of my first major career achievements, the team consisted of my fellow salespeople in the local office and the sales manager. These days, that notion (along with the quaint concept of water-cooler conversation) has fallen by the wayside. There is no office, per se. Salespeople can work with virtual, wireless, and Bluetooth ease from any corner of the world, perhaps seeing each other in the flesh only at a monthly meeting.

In my professional experience, successful people are seasoned team leaders more often than not. They have recognized that a chief limitation to achieving major success is trying to go it alone. The key, in fact, is to surround yourself with a team of smart people. I am especially amused that I, a C-plus student throughout my formal schooling, have A-plus students working for me today. The irony is not lost on me, I assure you.

Countless individuals excel at multitasking—that is a given. But the tradeoff is much less output than would be possible as a result of a cohesive team effort. Output is the volume, size, or scope of products or services to be produced. As you will hopefully learn in this chapter, output is crucial when it comes to team dynamics.

My personal definition of *team* is "two or more people united to achieve common goals." This may be a simple explanation, but scratch the surface and you will find layer upon layer of nuance. Who, specifically, are these people? Where are they to be found? And what are the team's specific tasks or goals? What about the individual role of each team member? Most important, who is leading the team? These questions hint at the vast complexity of team building. The success or failure of the team depends on the answers.

I've had the opportunity to work in Corporate America for twenty-plus years. What I observed is the importance of teams and team building. In Corporate America, the team is often led by a manager who must build a team no differently than a coach would build a team, no differently than a recording artist would build a team. The concept of team building remains constant across all cultures. Recently, in my downtime, I watched a special on the Seattle Seahawks. The topic was the coach—which in Corporate America or music would be the manager. This coach had a strategy to build the Seahawks team around players who had been journeymen, were passed over in the draft, or were drafted in at a very low draft number. He understood that psychologically these players would have a vengeance for success; they would work even harder to prove a point to those who had passed them over.

As I write this, it occurs to me that this could be one of the reasons Destiny's Child was so successful. The group encountered similar circumstances. Many record labels passed on Destiny's Child, including Atlantic Records and LaFace Records, to name a couple. When Destiny's Child finally got a major deal from Electra Records, they were subsequently dropped.

A key aspect of a team is that it is only as strong as its weakest member. Never forget that. I sold Music World Entertainment in 2002 to Sanctuary Music, the largest independent record label in the industry, to build an entire division called Music World/Sanctuary Urban, which consisted of a management company, record label, publishing, and merchandising. This concept is better known today as the *360-degree model*. I looked around the marketplace for managers and artists who I wanted to be on the team. I had two simple criteria: they had to have a desire to be the best, and they had to understand the team concept.

I am also intimately familiar with faulty team building. Almost daily in the music industry, I see singers and producers limit their success by surrounding themselves with all the wrong people. Incompetent friends are sometimes assigned central roles in the careers of breakout stars, believe it or not. And as reluctant as I am to confess it, I need only look in a mirror to identify an architect of a few screwed-up teams.

One that stands out from my early days? When I became president of Music World/Sanctuary Urban Records—the music label resulting from the sale of my company to the British recording giant Sanctuary—I put together my first team by trial and error. More often than not, I erred.

Why? I did not realize that I needed members with specialized skills—until it was too late, that is. I failed to recognize that certain pieces of the overall puzzle were missing, metaphorically speaking. That shortcoming only became obvious once the team began functioning (or rather, not functioning). And yet, this episode proved to be illuminating in that I learned a valuable lesson from it. Namely, that team-building skills can be gained—and sharpened—through years of experience. The more success you achieve with optimally operating teams, the more your confidence in cobbling them together grows.

Team leadership styles tend to vary. One popular approach that I have observed is top-down: the team leader assigns members the tasks to be tackled. Another approach—the one that happens to be my own personal style—is more collegial. The team leader presents the challenge and then empowers the team to participate in meeting the goal. I rely on the input of my team members when it comes to the challenges we face as an organization at Music World. After I gather their input, I can finalize the task for the team's implementation.

It is a natural inclination for team leaders to recruit people they know or people they believe to be like-minded. But that should not necessarily be the protocol, in my opinion. With the team leader's close supervision, clashing team members often produce the best answers, approaches, and results. An executive and friend who shall remain nameless practiced this style of interplay with his team members. He was, in fact, Sony Music's former North American chairman, who had day-to-day control over all the company's labels during the reign of Destiny's Child.

While running meetings related to my artists, he would sit in one of two chairs in his office and I sat in the other. A sofa was reserved for his senior executives from marketing, radio, A&R, and so forth. They would often get into heated disagreements—and occasional arguments—about a topic. And the chairman would only add fuel to the fire.

"Mathew, let's just step out for a minute," he would sometimes say. Once outside, the chairman would confide, "Hey, I just wanted to evaluate who's got the strongest argument. When we go back into my office, I want to see which person the others support." Since then, I have implemented the chairman's style. I recall one time when my two top executives at Music World were going after each other—savagely, no holds barred—over e-mail. Both of them later phoned me, but I refused to get in the middle of their disagreement. Instead, I joked, "Go on and beat each other until you're crazy." To a certain extent, you want to build a team where members feel comfortable with professional disagreements.

On the other hand, as much as I love and admire Sony Music's ex-chairman, he seemed to surround himself with yes-men. Make no mistake, I've seen the yes-man mantra all throughout Corporate America as well. Just bear with me as I share an example from the music industry. In fact, any industry can easily be substituted to fit this analogy.

Now, the Sony Music chairman's proclivity was clearly on display at executive lunches where unreleased music would be played for his approval. Despite the fact that the music would be cranked up to silverware-shaking decibels, the faces around the room typically remained blank. Then the chairman would chime in with his review: "Turn that shit off!" Not until that moment would his key lieutenants comment and simultaneously shake their heads in unison, "Oh, man. I didn't like it either." On the other hand, if the chairman liked the music, you had better believe that the rest of the room would sing its praises too.

I have seen this Yes-Man Syndrome, as I like to call it, on too many occasions. Eventually yes-men teams come back to haunt you because you will have a big blind spot—and you won't even see the disaster bearing down on you until it is too late. That is why you have to hire a team with enough professional integrity to tell you the worst news as quickly as possible, perhaps even more swiftly than on those occasions when the members have good news to share.

In the music business, the nature of the team has evolved quite a bit since the arrival of Destiny's Child. Back then, in the 1990s, artists and record labels were traditionally on separate (and sometimes competing) teams.

The label's group was a mix of bean counters, creative execs, dealmakers, promoters, marketers, and—at the top of the pyramid—the mogul or CEO. Meanwhile, the singer's team was typically assembled according to the would-be recording star's artistic and commercial goals plus their overall aspirations. At a minimum, an upstart artist's team would (or, ideally, should) have a career manager—for both Destiny's Child and Beyoncé, that was, of course, me—and an entertainment attorney. Depending on the scale of star power fueling it all, the team could swell exponentially, including full-time employees (publicists, agents, branding managers, business managers, and stylists, for instance) and a rotating lineup of outside collaborators.

With regard to the record business, the artists and label teams would appear to be on the same side. Realistically, though, the relationship was a situation of opposites that inevitably attract. Tension simmered constantly. Artists rarely cozied up to labels, seeing them as the necessary evil that gobbled down a too-big bite of riches from their recording career. Similarly, labels envied the massive hauls of cash that a hot artist could earn—and did not have to share—from concerts, merchandise, product endorsements, a film career, or all of the above. Labels would sometimes even withhold information, guided by the philosophy that what the artist's team did not know meant less work for the label's already overextended staff.

But how things have changed! Today, a team that does not include a social-media expert can count on remaining in obscurity. To the entertainment ecosystem, you are nobody if you don't blog, tweet, upload videos to YouTube, share tracks on SoundCloud, update your status on Facebook, and Instagram yourself into the hearts (and wallets) of

America. Self-promotion on social media has become an art form in itself—just ask Nicki Minaj. Back in the day, a publicist with contacts at MTV as well as the morning and late-night talk shows was about all any next-big-thing needed to secure adequate exposure. Of course, that was back when MTV played music videos instead of episodes of *Teen Mom*, *Teen Wolf*, and *Catfish*.

Just as significant is the profound shift in the nature of the team and, in turn, the tenor of artist-label relations. It reflects the rise of the 360 deal, which has become the standard for talent–record company contracts. In the simplest terms, these contracts essentially make artists and labels partners across the breadth of an artist's commercial endeavors—from live performances to Hollywood, Madison Avenue, and beyond.

The nucleus of the artist's team remains mostly intact. So does the composition of the label's team. But seamless relations between the two sides now are standard operating procedure. For all practical purposes, the once-separate teams are fully integrated.

An instinct for survival forced this fundamental change. Both sides feared potential extinction because of assaults on the industry from digital pirates, seminal changes in how fans consume music, and other modern marketplace disruptions. These days, ties between labels and artists are tighter than ever before. For example, former chairman of Interscope/ Geffen/A&M Jimmy Iovine and producer/artist Dr. Dre were hardly just in the music business together. They are also partners in Beats, the phenomenally successful headphones brand now owned by Apple.

Here is another glimpse into the newly cooperative relationship between label honchos and artists: In the 1990s and part of the following decade, Sony Music's former North American chairman would convene a weekly Wednesday update meeting where he would sit in a chair and talk about Destiny's Child and Beyoncé. But beginning around 2005, I took a seat at the table and shared the latest news about my artists. I thank that man for his insight. That was a sizable—and profound—shift. We ultimately had a bigger team and everyone was sharing information with the same goals all out in the open. This way, we were far more likely to score and win the game. At the end of the day, there was still a leader, just like a sports team has a captain. Not everybody can be the captain, but after the coin toss, the whole team runs out on the field.

The fuller dynamics of building a team are illustrated by the career of Karen Fondu, one of the world's top beauty executives. Karen was a rising star with L'Oréal, the global cosmetics behemoth, in early 2000 when she wisely wooed Beyoncé for one of my daughter's earliest endorsement deals. Beyoncé's budding superstardom appeared to be a flawless match for L'Oréal's youthful womanly appeal. And indeed it was, as time proved. Over more than two decades now, Beyoncé has grown into a lucrative, and probably the most famous, global ambassador for the brand. The association has been a boon for Beyoncé's brand as well.

As this marketing synergy flourished, Karen's star continued to rise in the corporate world. In 2008, she was promoted to president of L'Oréal Paris, the division directly associated with Beyoncé. The impressive results are a tribute to the team that Karen carefully assembled. Her particular forte? Matching the right team member to the appropriate task. This flair for talent deployment involves accurately surveying the skill set of each particular team member.

Granted, it can be challenging to assign the right task to the right person. It is one of the most important skills that a team leader can possess. Karen excelled at it because, like most strong team builders, she had a firm grasp of the demands of each role. She also had a sure eye for identifying the unique talents of her employees. Experience had honed this strength of hers over time. You see, Karen had hopscotched the management organizational chart of nearly every facet of the L'Oréal Consumer Products Group: L'Oréal Hair Care; L'Oréal Cosmetics (where she was vice president of sales); and Plenitude Skin Care, a product line that she helped launch.

I am an unlikely veteran of the beauty industry myself. In the early 1980s, my former wife and I opened a hair salon that grew to become one of the largest and most popular in Houston. What did I learn from that experience? A lot. When you have that many people—especially creative people—working together in a small setting, successful teamwork is absolutely critical. We had many employees interfacing with customers, so our staff had to be clear on what their individual roles were. It was imperative for team members to ensure that they met the expectations of both management and our harried customers.

I learned that a woman has two primary expectations upon entering a beauty salon: she wants to get the hell out of there in the shortest possible amount of time, and she had better emerge more beautiful than before. These considerations factored into the core of our ethos—and a crucial part of team building is embracing the management's corporate philosophy. For example, as a general rule, employees were not permitted to utter the phrase "my customer"; it was always "our customer" so as to reinforce the importance of the team. We formed a united front and figured out how to beat every potential challenge. For our clientele, the overall experience was attributed to the salon, and the ensuing buzz helped to quickly build our brand.

Over the years, I coined the phrase *the three-second rule*. Basically, it refers to the first three seconds after you meet someone. In those first three seconds, before they even speak, you form an opinion of people based on their body language, their stature, their dress, their swagger.

When I met Joe Campinell, then president of L'Oreal USA, Inc.'s consumer products group and L'Oreal retail, I knew within three seconds that he was a leader. At our first meeting, I could tell he was also gauging my ability to think broadly. The more we spoke, the more we jelled on the "big idea." We had a vision to build a team by adding scale. What I mean is our team would be comprised of everything from artists to the record label to the brand L'Oréal to *all* the working parts. That was our big idea.

I've done a lot of endorsement deals in my career in the arts—Mercedes-Benz, Walmart, Pepsi, American Express, Samsung, and many others. But unequivocally, in my entire career, when I consider the business relationship, the opportunities, the ability to think big and do things in unique ways, if I was putting together a dream team, Joe Campinell would sit at the head of the table.

Team building is a skill that has been essential to my success. I had quite a successful run, most recently with L'Oréal, where I worked twenty-five years to the day. I started June 30, 1986, and I finished on June 30, 2011. After I'd worked at L'Oréal for about three months, I was promoted to general manager of what was at the time L'Oréal's hair-care division.

Subsequently, we combined L'Oréal hair care with cosmetics and skin care, so I was the head of the entire L'Oréal brand. Then, around 1999, we acquired Maybelline, and eventually I became head of that brand. Around the same time, we acquired Softsheen-Carson, so I had three divisions and some very, very talented people working for me. These people knew how to run a business but needed direction and guidance, so that's how I built the team.

Mathew and I met in Los Angeles years ago when I was looking for spokespeople for the L'Oréal brand. I actually met Mathew and Beyoncé, and we decided that working together was a good idea for everyone. We put together a contract that would work for all concerned, and it still does. Beyoncé was, and continues to be, one of L'Oréal's premiere spokespersons.

A team is a group of people assembled to accomplish a goal or a task who share a common objective, but for me, it goes beyond that. People matter; the team members matter. You have to have the right kind of people on the team in order to achieve the goals of a company. My great opportunity was to have fine people who worked with and for me, each outstanding in his or her role, and that made all the difference in terms of being a successful team.

Honestly, without the right people, you can have a team that's very dysfunctional, which is what lots of companies are experiencing right now. So the idea is to have a team that works together—a team that understands both what's said and what's unsaid. They must be aligned with the same objectives that have been set for the business and have the same basic methods of accomplishing the objectives.

Additionally, the members must be skilled in the respective positions that they hold. There are heads of divisions—marketing, sales, finance, and manufacturing—and then all the people underneath them. In my situation, I had several thousand people who were under my management, and one of the important aspects of the L'Oréal company is to have the right people in the right place—people who understand what the goals and objectives are, who are driven to achieve those goals, and who do it in a way that makes everyone feel good about what they do for a living. That's the whole L'Oréal company philosophy.

The ability to assess people is important in team building. Though it takes a special eye to spot the right people, oftentimes team leaders make judgments very quickly about a team member's strengths and weaknesses. This quick assessment can be premature because many times you work with people where you might see something you consider a weakness, but in reality it's because you're assessing them in the wrong kind of way. It can take maybe six months to get a handle on the kind of team members who work for you. It's clearer and easier to honestly assess people once you've had some time to see how they think, how they act, their decision-making capabilities, and their experience. Though an initial impression is important, given a little time, your team will define itself more clearly.

There are all kinds of management talent in the world, but when it comes to team building, the one objective I always had was to find people who were smarter than I was, but who maybe didn't have quite the experience I had. I looked for people who could make a huge contribution to the business objectives because of their talent. I, then, had the ability to guide them, direct them, coach them, and help them achieve what we wanted to achieve as a business unit. So I think that's part of the team building process.

Building a good team also requires the ability to determine who among the members are the best leaders. A good senior manager must aspire to the goals and objectives defined by the company. Additionally, senior managers must be good at building, uniting, and inspiring their own teams. For example, if I have eight people reporting to me, and they each have twenty people reporting to them, they must also be very good at team building, and that's something that is not always easy to find. In a very fast-paced, high-pressure, major growth company like L'Oréal, this is sometimes difficult to assess if you're too far away from the second-level people. However, I had the opportunity to spend a lot of time with people below my direct reports, and as a result, I was able to get a feeling for how the team was operating within the first level, the second level, and even the third level.

Another important thing we did was a 360-degree evaluation. With this type of evaluation, I would evaluate the people who worked for me, and they would evaluate me. It was a way to understand what my own strengths and weaknesses were. For example, I would learn where I was providing the right direction to people, where I was collaborating successfully, and where I was decisive—all from a sales, marketing, financial, IT, and factory perspective. They had a chance to assess themselves and also a chance to assess the people who worked for them.

Each level of the company would participate in this type of reciprocal assessment. I found that all very helpful because after I'd been in management for a while, I knew what my strengths were, but sometimes I wasn't sure where I was falling short. It was helpful to hear more directly from the people I managed. The 360-degree evaluation was a very useful part of what we did at L'Oréal, and it's still a large part of the culture there today.

From HR to the top management, reciprocal evaluations help us understand what things are working, find the talent, and move the talent within the organization to a different role in order to take advantage of their financial, creative, or manufacturing ability or what have you. That is the culture of L'Oréal, and that made it a very special place to work.

A good team builder understands that there is both natural talent and talent that can be learned and cultivated. There are elements that can be learned, such as how to be a smart financial person or a smart salesperson. People can learn techniques for being better at what they do. Those are things that oftentimes team members learn from their bosses. If you are told that there's an area where you need to improve and you understand what it is, you can get guidance about how to improve on what you're doing and how to make yourself a better team member. You can learn how to work more closely with people who work for you and how to work across divisions.

Some people possess an innate ability. They are just much better at some things than others because it's kind of a natural thing for them. It's not something that can be easily defined. In fact, I was often asked about my team-building skills. I'm not sure I could explain it to anyone. It's just what I do. I guess I could try to define some rules, theories, elements, and factors, but frankly, it's just the person that I am. I am able to see it in other people too. So then it becomes that I find ways to reward people and to grow people and to give them more and more challenges and so forth, because I see in them a bit of what I see in myself, even if I can't perfectly define it.

There are many examples over the course of twenty-five years with L'Oréal where we saw people who weren't capable of building a team that could achieve goals and objectives together. Obviously, it's a problem that must be confronted. You have to have a discussion with the person about what the issues are because some people like to operate completely on their own; they have to be by themselves, and they want to do everything themselves.

The problem is, in a big company where you have many, many multiple objectives and multiple pieces of the business to run, you can't possibly do it without having a team working together, solving problems together. It's impossible. You can try, but you will not be successful.

The important part of being successful is recognizing the need for a team that shares the same goals and works hard to achieve them, a team that feels success as a team effort, and a team that doesn't dwell too long on a failure or two along the way. A great team will learn from each success and failure how to be better, more proficient, and more successful with each project and issue.

Few team-building roles demand more talent than that of the general manager of a professional sports team, particularly a franchise of the National Football League. In 2011, I had the opportunity to meet one such talented guy, Rick Smith, the general manager of my beloved hometown team, the Texans. I have always been fascinated with football, but I did not understand it to the degree that I do now thanks to Rick. I have become familiar with the many decisions and roles involved in building and operating a professional team. For instance, I had never realized that a team begins the preseason with a ninety-player roster that has to be whittled down to fifty-three by the start of the regular season.

Gaining insight into the relationship between the general manager, the coach, and the owner also was illuminating. I did not know that in some instances, the GM alone selects the draft picks and the coach inherits whatever players the manager chooses for him. In other organizations, the GM and the head coach work together to build a roster. I just loved learning how this young man, Rick Smith, has to be a politician, and how he needs to manage an incredibly large budget—hundreds of millions of dollars.

These leadership and team-building abilities are obvious upon meeting Rick in person; he radiates strength and confidence, as any good leader should. In one season several years ago, the Texans lost something like six games in the last two minutes of the game because of their defense and specifically because of two weak positions, cornerback and safety. Consequently, Rick realized that he had to go and build a whole new team from scratch. He also brought in another coach who had a different philosophy for the defense, which meant that Rick had to adjust and recruit players with that strategy in mind. To me, this endeavor seems positively mind-boggling, but knowing Rick as I do now, he probably didn't break a sweat, let alone lose a wink of sleep at night.

I cannot think about the meaning of the word team *outside the context of leadership. Every good team I have been on or simply observed all possessed great leaders. In my opinion, that is probably the most important attribute of a team: good leadership. The leadership has to define the team's overall goals, put a vision in front of the group, and then give team members the tools—and motivation—to move forward.*

Any team builder must possess a certain degree of competency in his or her field. Building a team requires the leader to be a person with intuition and, hopefully, people skills. Asking folks to embrace a universal goal above all else—including the ego-driven desire to stand out—means having the savvy and intelligence to explain the benefits of putting the greater good front and center. It is no secret that professional football players are extremely competitive by nature.

Team leadership is all about action, meaning I must actively build the team around a vision consisting of common goals. I alone must identify and articulate individual roles on the team. Each team member must comprehend his or her individual role. Accountability is an important component of team dynamics, which is one reason that clarity about roles is of utmost importance. A team leader has to articulate a clear expectation—and then hold people accountable. As a leader, I build a team by keeping in mind how I expect members to perform, assessing their strengths and weaknesses. Then I put them in the position that enables them to be most successful.

I always recognize folks on the team who are capable of ascending to leadership. I can identify a person who has sufficient people skills to make it as a manager. I can also identify the people who are worker bees. They have a work ethic that lets their actions speak for themselves. I believe that strong team builders possess certain inherent abilities. But a person can still learn to be a better leader if he or she is observant as well as competent.

Experience will inevitably help make a person better as a team builder. I should know, because I have been a leader my entire life. In high school, I was president of the student government and captain of the football team; in college, I was president of my fraternity's pledge class. Since it is something I have always been interested in, I've read a lot about the topic over the years. Sure, there are some things I think and do as a team builder that come naturally, but I do not discount anything I have learned by studying.

I also learned a lot from my idols of team building. Previously, when I worked with the Denver Broncos, I became a young executive after moving away from coaching and into the front office. To prepare for the job, I had the opportunity to participate in a graduate management program at the Stanford Graduate School of Business. There I became familiar with—and learned—some of the philosophies of Bill Walsh, the late, legendary coach of the NFL's San Francisco 49ers. Bill taught classes at the business school, as a matter of fact. In Denver, my management career began when the Broncos were coached by Mike Shanahan, and he was another idol of mine.

When it comes to motivators in my business—the sports industry—I also think of guys like the great Vince Lombardi. I have listened to their speeches again and again. I study guys like that. And again, I read extensively. One book I can strongly recommend is The Leadership Secrets of Colin Powell. *Similarly, I appreciate the perspective of John Maxwell, who also writes about leadership, because it comes from a spiritual perspective.*

Whether you are talking about a professional sports team, a business venture, or an organization, certainly there's a team-building aspect inherent to its success or failure. In turn, that relates to the leadership element or lack thereof.

In my job, the process of assembling the team that takes the field and the team that manages the franchise is one and the same. One is no more difficult than the other. And if you do not get both right, you will not last long in this business. What is the starting point for each? That would be the objective. Then it is vitally important to define the roles and goals for each and every team member.

From that standpoint, it is more straightforward to assemble a team for the field. The positions, or roles, are already clearly defined. There is the defensive cornerback, a quarterback, and so forth. On the other team in question, I know that I need a college director, a salary-cap administrator, and so on. Where it gets complicated in both scenarios is when I start to drill down in those roles and specify what I want from each team member. I have to keep in mind the general characteristics of people who I want to fill those positions. Aside from a strong and solid work ethic, they must have integrity, be consistent, and be honest. In my mind, these are characteristics that supersede any position.

Put simply, team building is part science, part art, and part experience. Scientific thinking is oftentimes a necessity, especially where statistics are concerned. Experience informs me about the approaches that tend to work best. There is also an art to managing a team, because it is partly about feeling—instinctively knowing when to make a change and consequently acting on that decision. Then, too, I must admit that a little luck always plays a role, whether one is superstitious by nature or not.

Finally, it takes a great deal of faith—and belief—in yourself and in your own particular process, whatever that might be.

In the celebrity-endorsement sweepstakes available to top recording stars and A-list actors, Kelly Rowland was not far behind Beyoncé on the roster of ambassadors for L'Oréal. In fact, L'Oréal set its sight more narrowly with Kelly and settled on her as the face of their African American hair-care line, Dark and Lovely. Since I was managing Kelly at the time, this deal resulted in my introduction to Candace Matthews, who was then president of Softsheen-Carson, a L'Oréal division. Candace, who left to become the chief marketing officer for Amway in 2007, is a team builder with few equals. This was immediately evident to me in her ability to team with us to appeal to African American women, which was the core audience for Destiny's Child as well as for Dark and Lovely. We understood one another's approach, respected what each of us brought to the table, and together achieved a new and common goal. Like millions of fans around the world, Candace believed Kelly was beautiful inside and out—the perfect embodiment of the Dark and Lovely brand. Candace could see that Dark and Lovely projected the positive image that I wanted Kelly to portray too.

L'Oréal's team worked in tune with ours to make sure everything meshed. We controlled the imaging, since my former wife and I had been hands-on with Kelly's upbringing and career grooming from the start. We even managed to synchronize all of our crazy schedules. I remember a Dark and Lovely event at a Walgreen's in Chicago that coincided with a stop along Destiny's Child's concert tour. Kids lined up around the block for the opportunity to meet Kelly, who was making a promotional appearance at the store. Candace ensured that both brand and sales teams were involved with making our partnership a success. The relationship helped boost Dark and Lovely sales, brand awareness, and popularity; similarly, it bolstered Kelly's own flawless image.

Naturally, my mother is my first role model of a team builder. I happen to be the youngest of eighteen—yes, eighteen—kids. My mother created a team that consisted of her own child army. When she spoke to any one of us, she made that child feel like the most important person in her life. She knew how to bring out the best in each of us. And as a result, she elevated the family as a whole to accomplish things that statistically we should not have been able to achieve. She contributed to my own understanding of people—who they are and how to bring out the best in everyone.

I believe that you need strong teams to be successful at anything—be it at work or at home. In the business world, where I have spent many years, you will need to compile a team to solve a problem most of the time. You will need the benefit of multiple perspectives that only a group of team members can provide. Teams can contribute a variety of potential solutions and then decide as a group on the best possible one. Throughout the years, I have become adept at building strong teams and understanding what it takes to be able to deliver things, knowing since childhood that I could not do it alone. I understood that I must surround myself with bright people and manage them in such a way as to inspire their absolute best.

How do I define team building? Yes, it does involve assembling a group of people to accomplish a task. But actually creating a successful team is far more complex than that. There is a difference between just putting a group of smart people together and having a high-performing team. A team that truly excels necessitates that the whole will be bigger than the sum of its parts. It goes without saying that the people on my team need to possess tremendous talent, and I utilize their skill sets to build off one other, allowing the overall output to be greater. Everybody has to be aligned to a single goal. And all the team members must bring out the best in each other.

It is impossible to have a strong team if the leader is weak. A leader has to have excellent communication and interpersonal skills aside from inner strength. A leader has to be able to provide direction and set high expectations to achieve that direction. A leader has to be skilled at evaluating talent quickly as well as inspiring and leveraging that talent. And if, by chance, there is someone who starts to derail the team, the leader must have that hard conversation immediately. That may be a tough decision to make. But it will be better for the entire team in the long term. Nothing is worse than having someone on the team who is a weak link. You cannot risk breaking the chain of command.

Team building improves with experience, even for people who are naturals. I am far better at building teams now—thirty years into my career—than I was in the first five years. You learn that it is important for everyone on your team to respect one another and what each individual brings to the party. I do not expect all of them to necessarily like each other or to become close friends and confidants.

For a team leader, I think this perspective only comes with maturity. It is not something that you can see right away—that your team members do not have to be just like you or be people you like necessarily. As you mature in your business career, you learn to look for people who are capable of delivering so that you can align them and drive them toward the goal. You have to be very self-aware to build a strong team. Most important, you have to be comfortable surrounding yourself with people who may be faster and smarter and better than you.

When teams fail, the leader deserves more of the blame than any one person or specific circumstance. A strong team leader should have been paying attention to how the team was operating. Strong leaders single out problematic issues to head off failure—that's called troubleshooting.

Team building, in my opinion, combines art and science. You hear about EQ, or emotional intelligence, that a leader needs to run a team with expertise. EQ is what the team leader needs to possess so that ideas and skills of people with extremely high intelligence come together in a way that is leveraged for the greater good.

At Amway, I am experiencing team building in a whole new way. We have team members across international timelines, all completely opposite my own normal office hours. On top of time differences, there are cultural barriers as well. In some Southeast Asian countries, for example, team members will not debate publicly, because it is outside the norm of their culture. That is not a problem for Americans, as everybody knows.

This brings me to my second role model for team building, Richard DeVos, one of the cofounders of Amway. Obviously, I was not here when he launched the company with Jay Van Andel, who died in 2004 at the age of eighty. But I have had the opportunity to observe Rich DeVos build teams. He showed me how to transcend cultures, languages, and other likely obstacles. He not only built a strong team; he built a global enterprise. It is, in fact, the biggest team that you can imagine—an international network of people working together in harmony.

The difficulty I have recalling when exactly I first met certain successful music folks is a constant reminder of how a couple of extraordinarily eventful decades in the industry can seem like a big blur. However, of this I am certain: From the 1990s and into the current century, Neil Portnow, president of the National Academy of Recording Arts and Sciences (NARAS), thrived as a top executive team member of Jive Records, which launched blockbuster breakout acts like Britney Spears, 'N Sync and the Backstreet Boys, to name a few.

In late 2002, Neil traded in his music executive's suite for the reigns of NARAS, the official industry cheerleader for artistry, unparalleled musicianship, and cultural relevance. Established in 1957, NARAS grew out of an effort by promoters of the Walk of Fame to identify music-industry figures deserving of their own stars on Hollywood Boulevard in Los Angeles. Today, thousands of musicians, producers, and other NARAS members nominate their peers for Grammys in a wide variety of diverse categories. "Within the music business, Mr. Portnow is known as an organized, unflamboyant and relatively buttoned-down figure," the *New York Times* wrote in reporting on Neil's appointment as NARAS president.

Overlooked in that profile was Neil's genius at team building, which should be the chief qualification of anyone in that dizzyingly complex role. Just to mount the annual awards—the Oscars of the music industry—requires the NARAS president be a team-making maestro. Neil does not hesitate to sing the praises of team-building skills. "There is no substitute for having a great team," he likes to say.

That has been my conclusion about the operation of NARAS since 2001, when Destiny's Child first performed on the live telecast. After belting out a medley of their hits "Say My Name" and "Independent Woman," they took home the gold in the form of two Grammy Awards. Three years later, with the Music World Entertainment team behind her, Beyoncé arrived at the 2004 ceremony—the second one under Neil— with six nominations for her debut solo album, *Dangerously in Love*. She won five. Now she had the opportunity to make history with the most Grammys of any female artist. I absolutely believe that, within a few years, she will.

Two or more people coming together to achieve one goal—that is a starting point for the definition of team building. Certainly that is the most basic and simple universal way to define it. But once you get around to delegating the team's tasks, some further elaboration of that definition is required.

I believe that team-building talents are undoubtedly innate for most longtime leaders with a successful track record. But some related skills need to be learned over time. There are certain personalities that gravitate toward operating in leadership roles. On the other hand, there is no shortage of books, classes, and seminars that focus on improving leadership and team-building abilities. From time to time at the recording academy, we have been known to utilize career counselors who work with executives to help them fine-tune those kinds of ideas and principals. Yes, team-building talents can be learned, but that requires a sincere willingness and desire for self-improvement.

At the core of this concept—in my mind at least—is the belief that two heads are always better than one. Secondly, it is important for any team leader to recognize what he or she does not know but needs to learn. Then, by definition, you are talking about more than one person in the room. This helps create a mind-set and an ability to work with others, including others who happen to know more than you do.

Acknowledging that team members may know more than you, their leader, is a problem for some people, though not for me. When people get stuck on that issue, it is because of the ego. You must simply accept that you are not an expert in every single area. Some people are uncomfortable and insecure when it comes to acknowledging that fact.

For a confidence-challenged leader, not knowing as much as a member of the team can become a serious control issue. Whenever a team member knows more than an insecure leader, it may be difficult for that leader to feel like he or she still has complete control of the group. You have to trust your team enough that you are comfortable entering areas where you may not have any expertise—or experience, for that matter.

In the mind of a team leader who is lacking self-confidence, fear plays out in this faulty logic: if a team member knows more than me, isn't my management position in jeopardy? But it takes total faith in the team to rely on someone else's judgment in order to meet the leader's goals. In group training, the following exercise is sometimes recommended: An individual is surrounded by fellow team members. That individual is then instructed to literally fall backward—and to rely on team members to catch him or her. These are the kinds of trust and comfort factors that a team leader needs to achieve.

Lack of willingness to assemble the best minds that one can find is something that I see from time to time. And it is always unfortunate. If you have a roomful of folks who know what you don't—and are really smart and passionate about the task at hand—their combined wisdom will give you the best odds of achieving the desired goal. Whereas if leadership is ego-driven rather than collaborative, opportunities for success will be missed no matter how smart the team leader is. Even geniuses are wrong sometimes.

After ten years as the head of the recording academy, I certainly believe that my focus on team building has resulted in many success stories. If you compare the organization today to the way it looked when I first started, it is vastly different—and for the better. Obviously, I cannot be totally objective about that. But the feedback I get suggests that we have taken the recording academy to whole new level. In my humble opinion, that happened because

I have been able to identify a vision of where we wanted to be and helped guide my team to achieve that lofty goal.

After all, the first thing I sought to do on day one was create the most extraordinary team of people I could find. It involved taking some of the best minds that were already here at the recording academy, finding the weak links, making the necessary changes, and then bringing in a new cast of exceptional people. As a result of that remixed team, NARAS is now in a position that it has never been in before—and the sky is truly the limit.

Every year at the height of the madness that is Grammy week—and with everything riding on seven days in February—some people will say to me, "You look relatively calm and under control. How do you deal with the pressure?" My answer is this joke: "Well, it's the medication." But the real answer is that I do not lose any sleep. I do not worry, because I believe that cannot fail. My team consistently delivers. These are people who will go to the ends of earth to make sure that everything goes according to plan. As for the things that are out of our control—what the weather will be like for the red carpet on the day of the big show, for example—we can't change that anyway.

Quiz: Team Building

Below is an exercise I used to do with Destiny's Child back in the day. In this challenge, you should learn that when it comes to team building, it is all about the team—and that one of us will never be as strong as all of us working together.

1. Pretend that you and several of your friends have been given the following challenge: Everyone place a book on the ground in front of him or her and then stand on it with both feet. Imagine that all of you are standing in a straight line with your arms extended so that your fingertips touch the hands of the team member next to you. Now at the opposite side of the room, envision a finish line. The goal is for your team to get to the opposite side of the room without anyone

stepping off his or her book. If someone falls off a book, the entire team has to start over again. Ready? Go!

2. How would you plan to get across the room without falling down?

3. Would you offer to help your fellow team members? If so, how?

4. Who would be the first of your friends to get across the imaginary line?

5. Reflect on your answers and ask yourself, "Am I truly a team player?" If you answer no to this question, I suggest reading this chapter over again!

5

Planning

It's difficult to imagine that an airline pilot would be as clueless as a baby and yet still settle into the cockpit. Really, what pilot in his or her right mind wouldn't want to confidently know beforehand how to navigate an aircraft from point A to point B? But winging it wasn't all that uncommon in the early days of aviation, back in the 1930s.

There is one legendary episode of a pilot flying off half-cocked. Aviation buffs know well the tale of aviator Douglas Corrigan. In 1938, he piloted himself into infamy for all time by flying his plane from Brooklyn, New York, to Ireland instead of the destination he supposedly had in mind—Long Beach, California. On a story about the incident, one local newspaper, the *Edwardsville Intelligencer*, ran this headline: "Corrigan Flies by the Seat of His Pants."

History will show that suspicion surrounds Corrigan's errant flight. He might not have been so in the dark about the fact he was flying opposite his intended direction—a feat of bumbling that earned him the nickname "Wrong Way Corrigan." Still, the truth is, pilots had little choice but to fly by the seat of their pants in those days, relying on their gut and any prior experience aloft for guidance along a flight path. Today, the Federal Aviation Administration requires every pilot to file a flight plan that includes such vital information as departure and arrival points, duration of flight, route, numbers of passengers, and navigational procedures. Flying by the seat of the pants is a thing of the past—at least in cockpits.

How does this then-and-now snapshot of aviation relate to the planning trait that many successful people have in common? Everything. I've never encountered a successful person who flew by the seat of the pants to reach his or her happy fortune. Of course, people who aspire to be successful aren't required by any regulatory agency to have a plan. But the successful people I know all believe that planning is essentially along the flight path to success. They all have a flight plan of some sort. And for most, the need for a plan was self-evident from the very beginning of their journey.

To gain a deeper understanding of this trait—and to improve my own planning skills—I've specifically talked with many of my successful acquaintances about this topic. Almost to a one, they never stopped trusting their gut. They deemed it crucial to have a method and a strategy to parlay their gut instinct into an achievable outcome. Trying to decide a course of action en route wouldn't cut it for them. None rode guesswork to the top of the heap.

Not surprisingly, the most pervasive context for planning seems to be our jobs. How we earn a living has such far-ranging effects on our lives that we naturally tend to be more deliberate in going about it. If you have spent a day employed by Corporate America, you know that planning is a core discipline of business. I had the good fortune of working for Xerox in the 1970s, when it was one of the nation's best corporations.

Xerox was all about making sure that we were always prepared with a plan of action. I went through the training sessions designed to sharpen our skills at strategizing.

That was not the case when I left behind the corporate world and joined the girls on their rise to the top of show business. In the music industry, shooting from the hip is the modus operandi. Folks just don't plan realistically. They make quick work of it and don't truly think things out. The diagnostic imaging field in which I also worked is the extreme opposite. When you are dealing with human lives, timelines, billions of dollars at stake, and the Food and Drug Administration hovering over your shoulder, guess what: you make plans. Mistakes can delay product introductions. Rivals race ahead of you. Stockholders want answers.

So too is strong planning essential in the apparel industry, where we had success with House of Deréon, Beyoncé's and her mom Tina's ready-to-wear fashion line. They had to be really on top of planning to meet deadlines for four distinct seasons. Almost a year in advance, each seasonal fashion line has to be produced; at this point in my writing of this book, heading into winter, the fashion industry is designing for next summer. That was a steep learning curve for me. It involved sourcing in Asia, licensing different categories of product (shoes, accessories, furs, apparel), and identifying the licensees. It also required intense planning and coordinating with retailers. We were fortunate to build three brands—House of Deréon, Deréon, and Miss Tina—all of which required strategic planning. I quickly learned that the end goal of the strategic planning process was to position the company to be sold, which we did eventually to Li & Fung.

Aside from the girls' raw talent, what made the ride successful in entertainment? We devised a plan for Destiny's Child. First, everyone in the music business was describing it as just that—a *business*. In our planning, however, we conceived of music as just the nucleus of our pursuits. We thought in terms of the entertainment industry, not just the music industry. As a result, our planning strategy included opportunities beyond music, including branding, apparel, and other product offerings.

Our strategy for leveraging the core music component was quite evident from the start—female empowerment. You have these three independent women, so they were talking about female authority, perspective, and liberation. What did we do to extend that positioning to other arenas and opportunities? One example: in 2000, we partnered with filmmakers for the soundtrack of *Charlie's Angels*, the movie adaptation of the hit TV series of the same name. Like Destiny's Child, the film featured three women, and in a way it also was about female empowerment.

The results couldn't have been more successful. Destiny's Child's lead single, "Independent Women," which was co-written by Beyoncé, soared to number one on the Billboard 100, where it remained for eleven weeks. And it anchored the group's third studio album, *Survivor* (2001). The movie opened at number one at the box office and the album opened at number one. That was a strategy, not luck.

Another strategic plan of Destiny's Child was that each member would individually pursue her artistic love as a recording artist. Michelle, coming from a church background, chose gospel. Kelly, with her international appeal, chose pop. And Beyoncé, as we all know, chose pop/R&B. Destiny's Child would make an album, and then each of the ladies would individually release her own album, thus building the audience and the brand of Destiny's Child. This is a strategy we repeated, and it now allows each of the ladies to freely exercise her career in the hope that one day a new Destiny's Child album, tour, and movie will transpire.

I can't say that everything I do involves a plan. But for most things, I do try to have a plan of action. It helps me be clear on my direction and how I'm going to reach my destination. Chances are I won't get there otherwise. But plans aren't—or should not be treated as—sacred and static. Sometimes we don't get a plan right the first time. Sometimes we have to modify our initial approach. Tracking results, an important element in the planning process, is often overlooked, according to the successful people I've observed. Yet it's essential to take a measure here and there along the way toward your goal. Otherwise, you can't assess your progress with any confidence or know whether the overall plan is working.

Plans may need to be tweaked as a result of changing circumstances in the marketplace. For years, radio play was the way we measured success in the music industry. Then along came social media, which could have an instant measureable impact on the ultimate success of a song or artist. Before social media, TV became an important medium in building a music career. Successful people are always open to the shifts that can happen in marketplaces. They are always poised to quickly change plans and strategies. The key word is *quickly*. I predict the next change will be the importance of video.

It's a good idea to actually write your plan. It need not be elaborate and long. But just the idea of typing it out helps discipline you to think methodically about what you intend to achieve. It can also help you identify your strengths and weaknesses. For entrepreneurs looking to attract investors, a formal business plan is mandatory. In deciding whether to bet on entrepreneurs, investors and lenders understandably want to see and be convinced that there's a clear step-by-step pathway to success.

I don't know any successful people who just stumble upon success without planning. Hope wasn't their approach to becoming successful. They didn't bet on simply being in the right place at the right time. It doesn't happen that way. I read recently about the plight of lotto winners. A high percentage end up right where they started—with nothing. Although luck brought them fortune, maintaining their windfall proved to be impossible because they didn't have a plan. Nor did they have the opportunity to observe the kind of master planners I've been fortunate to know, such as the three successful gentlemen you will meet next.

Although Ken Ehrlich is one of the most skillful planners I know, he doesn't let his strength at planning overwhelm his instincts. He sees planning as an art—something to be balanced with a measure of spontaneity, as he puts it. I realized his ability to balance was one of his strong suits early in our relationship. Just like so many successful folks I've been fortunate to meet, I can't recall the exact beginning of our ties.

It was likely a gargantuan televised event—the MTV Awards, Live 8, or the Grammys (which he has produced since 1980). These are Ken's specialty. Destiny's Child and Beyoncé as a solo act have done several shows produced by Ken. He and I have never spent a whole lot of social time together, but we've had many strategic planning breakfasts at the Regent Beverly Wilshire Hotel.

Aside from his great success as a major behind-the-scenes fixture in entertainment, Ken is one of the industry's good guys. From the beginning, he was willing to indulge my desire to soak up as much knowledge as possible. Each time I saw him, he would notice the additional level of show-business expertise I'd gained in the interim. He seemed to respect that in me—that I didn't know everything and was vocal about saying how much I wanted to learn. And when it comes to insight into the planning trait, there are few better to observe than Ken.

There's a tremendous amount of planning that goes into monster shows like the Grammys. I start a year ahead, working on staffing. There are definitely certain elements that are long term. There are certain ducks to get in order. There are scripts that need to be written. Nominees need to be seated here, there, or wherever. We can't really book the show performers until the nominations come out. So we focus on what we can plan in order to meet the expectations of the audiences that watch the Grammys or other event-type programming from year to year. Viewers know a number of people will sing and a number will appear to accept awards and give thank-yous. They'll hear a lot of music that they're familiar with and expect when they come to watch these shows. Our shows in particular will have surprises and introduce them to things they don't know.

So the planning for a show like this is that we know what the overall look will be. We work on a master of the set. We have to build a stage. That's kind of a flat forty-by-eighty-foot bunch of boards supported from the floor of the arena. It's what you do after the stage is in place. That's not what people want to watch the show for. They want to know what's going to be on that deck. They want to know what the colors are—not the literal colors but the figurative colors, the creative colors.

To me, the magic of what we do is having everything seem as though it's not planned out. You never really want to lose the spontaneity of the moment.

Maybe the only way you can adapt is by having a good plan in mind when you're going into something. Even with those shows, I think what I've learned—and I've produced the Grammys for thirty-one years now—is that planning takes you only so far. You need to allow for a certain amount of change, shift, and spontaneity.

In this particular business, you're working with an incredibly volatile and changing element—talent. Creativity isn't counter to planning. But you can't lock yourself in too much when you know the people you're working with are pretty changeable. Your mind needs to be incredibly open to other people's ideas. If the plan is working, stick with it throughout the project. But I think everybody is in the same boat, particularly in the entertainment industry, and has to be ready for shifting.

This past year, I directed Celine Dion's Las Vegas show. The kind of shows that I usually do air once. We can spend two, three, or four months on it for a year, and then it airs, and it's done. You can't change it once it happens. But with a show like Celine's, which opened in 2011 to great reviews and is going to be there for a number of years, you go into it with a little different thinking. You hope that the show you put up on opening night is the show that people love and is going to be there. But you also know that it can definitely evolve. The sensibility is that, if it doesn't work, you can change it.

I can't help but think that I'm not much of a planner when I consider the paths that my career has taken. Life is a combination of being directed and of being driven. Most successful people I know are driven. I think that generally successful people will come to forks in the road where they can take a chance. I've had two or three of those things that led me to this day, forty-odd years later. The first came when I was living in Chicago, out of college for a couple years, and starting my career in public relations at a black jazz station with a white Jewish DJ who got his start in TV. All of a sudden, he was going back on television. And out of nowhere, he asked me to come and produce his show, which I'd never done before. That was a fork. At that point, I could have said, "I'm not ready ... blah blah." And my life never would have been changed. That was the moment that kind of launched me into the world of television.

Another turning point came four years later, when this country was in the Vietnam War. There was a lot of turbulence in Chicago, where we lived in the inner city. I was offered a job at my alma mater, Ohio University in Athens, Ohio—a good position in the development and fundraising department. The short story: Literally the day before (Friday, and the movers were coming Saturday), a friend at the local PBS station called and asked if we could have lunch. From lunch, we went to her station, where I met new guys who'd just taken over running the station. They offered me a job then and there, to be involved in PR, fundraising, and programming—creating shows. This was long before cell phones. I remember stopping at a phone booth and calling my wife to say, "We're not going to Athens." That led to, about four years later, an opportunity to come out here to Los Angeles.

Neither of these were planned. They were instinctive responses to opportunities that were offered. I could have said no to either of them. Whatever success I've found was helped by my ability to recognize opportunities, even though a certain amount of risk was involved, to move forward and take a chance.

That doesn't mean I don't set goals, which is a first step in planning. I think most people who do what I do set goals. Again, and not counter to what I said before about how my career has unfolded, I think we all kind of have our eyes on the prize. I think the prize can change from time to time.

Where entertainment, luxury hotels, and iconic events converge, you will find Jerry Inzerillo. "Anywhere and everywhere" is how I think of his presence across the recent decades. We were introduced by Tommy Mottola, then CEO of Sony Music, and Quincy Jones, a mutual acquaintance. So from the beginning of Destiny's Child up through Beyoncé's surge to the top, I have known him.

By Jerry's count, he's conceived and produced more than nine hundred major events worldwide. He launched Atlantis Resorts in the Bahamas and Dubai, both star-studded openings, when he was president of Kerzner Entertainment Group. The countless hotels he has launched include the most respected branded chains in the industry—Kerzner International, One&Only Resorts, Ian Schrager Hotels (where he was founding president), and Four Seasons and Hilton.

Who he doesn't know may be a shorter list than who he knows. None other than Nobel Peace Prize Laureate Archbishop Desmond Tutu asked him to coordinate Nelson Mandela's presidential inauguration. At the groundbreaking of properties for Schrager Hotels, he mingled with a who's who of celebrities at the Royalton, Paramount, and Delano.

Since 2012, he's been chief executive officer of IMG Artists, one of the world's major managers of performing artists and lifestyle events. He's a masterful planner, and he's a natural at taking the devil out of the details.

If someone asked me what was my personal favorite event to plan over a forty-year career, it would be Nelson Mandela's inauguration when he became South Africa's first black president in 1994. It was one of my most complex planning exercises ever because it involved directing many disciplines at the same time: security, protocol, logistics, press, and VIPs. I remember a major lesson learned from the inauguration: how to plan for the unexpected and avoid surprises at showtime on the day of the event.

Contingencies allow you to keep cool under pressure. No stressing out or collapsing if plan A doesn't work out. The Mandela inauguration included a banquet with 1,400 guests. Diplomatic protocol was very, very complex, especially around seating. In the back of the marquee, I stashed five tables of ten, fully set with china, silverware, glasses, and linen, just in case an ex-head of state showed up out of the blue. Which actually sort of happened. The president of Nigeria arrived unexpectedly. All of a sudden, there are three top Nigerian officials—the current president and his two predecessors. You can't say, "Mr. President, you can't come in." So you'd better have a plan. What to do? Add a table from the back. What to say? "Oh, we were expecting you." No one knew the difference.

The old saying goes, "Success is never certain, failure never final." But still, I find there's an extremely disproportionate amount of success directly attributable to proper planning than not so.

When did I realize that planning would be central to who I'd become? Some people are experts at seat-of-the-pants. I've never been that person. I like to win. I like to succeed. But I never was the fastest kid in the class, so I had to prepare more to beat the best kid in class. And a lot of times I did beat the best kid because my preparation exceeded my own raw talent. Of course, other human characteristics—tenacity, perseverance, faith, and will—go into the equation. But in the context of how I succeeded in the classroom, I found early in life that planning works very well.

You hear entrepreneurs saying they had no plan, that they saw an opportunity and seized it. That is more urban legend than fact. Do I know anyone who didn't plan and had accidental success? Most business schools cite the example of Colonel Harland David Sanders, who at sixty-five or sixty-six decided to take some of his chicken recipes and open a restaurant. Next thing you know, he's created Kentucky Fried Chicken.

I come from the school that says very little success is accidental. At some point along the way, the most successful brands and businesses in the world had a methodical and detailed plan. At Apple, Steve Jobs was not only a conceptualizer and a visionary; he was a methodical planner. Did one of my great heroes, Isadore "Issy" Sharp, founder and chairman of Four Seasons Hotels, plan a hundred-hotel chain when he and his father opened the first Four Seasons in the 1960s? No, he didn't. But his vision to have one great hotel after another was rewarded with success.

Howard Schultz probably didn't plan for Starbucks to get as big as it has—a worldwide organization, transcending all cultures. Quincy Jones was superb at planning. This is the guy who was able to write original music scores, do films, and make records. He couldn't have influenced multiple genres without everything being well planned and well thought-out.

At some point, all of these great entrepreneurs decided that to get to the next level, they would need a plan. They had to change their strategic formula to allow their companies to grow. I don't know too many people who had accidental success.

Planning does not guarantee you an outcome. The more you anticipate in advance, the more you plan, the greater control you have over the uncertainty. Planning is important, especially when the outcome of any particular situation may not be controllable. Planning guarantees you a higher percentage of success because you can define, identify, and manipulate the variables of what you are trying to accomplish.

A good rule of thumb for planning out an exercise, even the most complex and multifaceted—multiple people, disciplines, countries, tasks—is to think of how you put together a thousand-piece jigsaw puzzle. Before you begin actually putting it together, you plan your approach: step 1, border; step 2, dominant image; and so on from there.

Be methodical, but not to the point of driving creativity out of your people or their ability to contribute. It's not my way or the highway. Planning is a discipline, not a suppression of creativity or initiative. Simple things require less planning. You can go on experience and instinct. The word I tend to focus on is outcome—*what is your outcome? Until you know your desired outcome, the planning process doesn't budge. You can't plan for an unknown outcome.*

If the best-laid plan works, great! Share the credit. If it doesn't work, you have to be able to maneuver very quickly out of it to the proverbial plan B. The minute you see that everything you planned is not going well, you must be able to move laterally into a different strategy. Very successful entrepreneurs, unlike big bureaucratic organizations, have the ability to adapt to a failed plan or a plan that didn't meet expectations quickly.

Eastman Kodak, I think, is one of the great cases of not adapting your plan. When we were growing up, Kodak was generic for camera and film, like Xeroxing used to be for copying. Now Kodak is not even a player anymore— because they forgot to adapt and plan. Kodak didn't realize that photography was no longer about pictures. It was about images. They took their eye off the ball. And I think that's poor planning.

While the best-laid plans of mice and men may sometimes go awry, when Colin Cowie is in charge, you can almost bet the house that nothing will go wrong. This guy is the planning guru. As a party planner extraordinaire, he is one guy who is never short of ideas; he is as proficient at entertaining Oprah Winfrey's five hundred closest friends (he masterminded her daytime TV farewell extravaganza) as he is at accommodating something smaller-scale at his swanky penthouse in Manhattan.

I've witnessed many of Colin's events firsthand. I know that his productions are first-class. I know that he is the embodiment of calm, cool, and collected under pressure. I also know that his staff reflects the same essence in their demeanor. And I know why: because they understand the importance of planning.

When I was a young boy in South Africa, we had a black-and-white television, and I always used to love seeing images of the Hollywood sign. Even at four or five years old, I knew that I wanted to go to Hollywood. As I got older and began to understand the world and politics, more and more I didn't believe in the political system in South Africa—apartheid. I felt very oppressed. I didn't want to spend all of those years in what I thought was one of the most challenged countries at the time. I didn't know what the future looked like, so as a result, I emigrated to New York.

I arrived in the United States in 1985 with four hundred dollars and a plan. I guess my biggest challenge was that because I was so young, people didn't think I was capable of doing all the things that I said I could do. But because I was raised to be a hardworking South African, I came through every single time. Because I had a dream and a plan, and because I could produce, I met the right people at the right time.

My first big break came at Hugh Hefner's wedding. I was taking a cooking class and the woman who was teaching the class, her husband was the president of Playboy. She invited me to be a food consultant for Hefner's wedding event. I took one look at the menu and the magnificent property and said to them, "If I were to do it, this is what I would serve, and this is how I would present it, and this is how I would decorate."

It got bigger and better. Eventually, the president of Playboy came to discuss my ideas, and half an hour later, I was speaking to Hugh Hefner in his pajamas. He asked me, "Can you do this? The wedding is in six weeks' time."

I absolutely, categorically, had no clue in my mind how I was going to do it, but to this day, it was probably one of the most thoroughly produced events I ever created. That's because I had a plan—an organized, flexible, well-executed plan. It's a funny thing. Always be careful what you pray for, wish for, and plan for. I mean, it's amazing that I went from four hundred dollars in 1985 to planning these weddings that cost millions.

Success for me means recognition by my peers, having a recognizable brand, and running a profitable company with the ability to expand and to leverage. It also means having pride in my work. I strive and plan every morning when I wake up to be the best version of myself, whether I'm at home, at work, or just having fun.

The formula I adhere to in order to achieve at such a high level most definitely includes having a detailed plan and putting real resources behind it. Those resources must keep the profits up, keep the overhead down, and adjust with the market. Everything is so interconnected today, and the way that information is accessible to everyone has completely changed the way that we do business. Now the playing field is even for everyone.

Ten years ago, there was a handful of us who controlled all the resources. The average bride couldn't find the band or the DJ or that great decorator, so we were able to charge a premium for our services. Today, anyone can Google anything and get the information, so the middleman or the designer is taken out of the equation. The market in the service industry has changed completely.

The design is the easy part of the equation. Anyone can do that. The difficult part is the execution. When you deal with the clients that I deal with, most of them are self-made, which means they're exceptionally smart people.

They know how to do things. They know how to get things done, so because I never want to start a conversation with "I'm sorry," I have to make sure that my organization runs and operates like a Swiss watch. We must have the ability to pivot on a dime and be agile should something not work. Then, if and when something's not working, I've surrounded myself with the smartest people to be able to make sure that there's never any negative impact on the product or the brand.

My event planning is intricate, with many parts to it. I keep thinking of Atlantis, when we not only had fireworks going off in the windows of the hotels but we also had Janet Jackson performing. Just at the opening event, we had 25,000 flowers, 10,000 pieces of sushi, 11,000 shrimp, 2,000 pounds of lobster, 3,000 oysters, 10,000 shots of tequila, 27,000 pieces of silverware, food displayed on walking buffets, spectacular women adorned with costumes, and tables featuring delectable treats and cocktails. As the sun set, Janet Jackson made her grand entrance with a series of spark showers and a giant marquee that was set ablaze to spell out "Janet," followed by fireworks at the conclusion.

When you have these kinds of variables, what's amazing is that everything goes off without a hitch, because I plan every detail. It's all thought through, with tons and tons of production scheduled. At the end of the day, it's like producing a Broadway show; the only difference is you only get one night, one chance to do it. So when I'm hired to produce something like Janet Jackson performing in Dubai—which was the largest project in the history of the world, by the way—at any particular moment there may be eighteen different cues. We are dealing with lights, with sound, with performers, with pyrotechnics, with video projection, with personnel, and add to that food, servers, etc., and so when I call a button for 659, 715, 720, 722 cue, even with all these different disciplines, they have to respond on their particular cue.

That is the ultimate. It is a tremendous amount of responsibility on my shoulders at each and every one of these events. If something doesn't happen or it happens out of line or it happens out of cue, nobody looks good. I can't even describe the stress level. It's like directing an epic musical, an epic movie on a regular basis, and you have to depend on all of these other people to hit their cues. That is why planning is essential to success. At that level, no one wants to have to say "I'm sorry" to the client when they bought and paid for the best.

I surround myself with the most dedicated team, and we've spent twenty years planning and replanning, writing and rewriting, tuning and fine-tuning standard operating procedures to find new and better ways to produce an event. We do a complete spot analysis. We figure out what are the strengths, what are the weaknesses, what are the opportunities, and what are the threats. That way we're sure to learn from each event, so we get better next time around.

That said, every now and again, something comes back to bite you in the ass. No matter how good you are, it's a function of life, and it's how we learn. We all experience ups and downs. But if they approach all the lessons and embrace them, they'll never be failures. No matter how painful it is, if you can pivot and be agile, you will progress, grow, and develop. It's only when things are uncomfortable, sticky, and painful that we really get to learn our lessons.

The events I create are like high art, and they have grown over the years into these unique, extravagant, and extraordinary visions because of the intense amount of planning I've done for each one. Because of my ability to plan ahead and see things through, I've been an innovator of design and idea production. I've started a lot of trends in our business. For example, when we first started projecting on the exteriors of buildings, using buildings as a backdrop, we projected pictures of Arnold Schwarzenegger, Stallone, Melissa Etheridge, and Samuel Jackson smoking cigars. The next minute, people were smoking cigars all over the place.

Because so many people are interested in my event planning and my success at planning, I've written some successful books. I've published nine books, with the tenth book on the way. I launched my very first book about eighteen years ago on Oprah's show. I remained friends with Oprah, and I started doing parties and events for her. Then Oprah and I did lectures together and then a reading club. In the meantime, I'm on her show fifteen or twenty times, with even an entire one-hour special for me. I've had an incredible journey with her, and I'm one of the few people she trusts implicitly.

She knows that because I intricately plan, I will always, always produce a tremendous event.

As a result of this influential association and reputation, I have been able to leverage my brand and enjoy credibility with celebrities. Those celebrities become the covers of the magazines, and so for me that is an opportunity to sell my brand through china, florals, silver, or crystal. Next came my own television show, Everyday Elegance; *then the Home Shopping Network, where I've been a fixture for seven years. I've worked as creative director for NetJets and Hotel Miramar in Hong Kong. I have a very great, very exciting business doing lots of exciting things, but at the end of the day, it all comes back to what I love to do most, and that's planning—planning large events.*

I still feel like there is more for me to achieve. I don't yet feel like I want to rest on my accomplishments. I actually work so hard and I run at such a pace that when it comes time to pat myself on the shoulder or tell myself how great I've done and how fabulous I am, I'm always working on the next thing. There's always more to do, so I still look at myself and my sleeves are rolled up. I haven't even begun to do what I've set out to do. I'm fifty-one years old, and yet I feel my life is just beginning. My greatest work, I believe, is still ahead of me.

My plan for the future is to continue to both grow and develop Colin Cowie Celebration and to make it a national company where we've got offices in other cities. I have a new television show starting in the next year, and Colin Cowie Weddings continues to grow and develop. We are number one on the Web, so now we're going to take this business global.

How do I have all of this? Because I started with a plan. I had a plan from the beginning, and it still works for me today.

Quiz: Planning

1. Carefully define what you would like to accomplish.

2. Set very specific goals.

3. What is a reasonable time frame for achieving your goals?

4. What tools are needed to reach your goals?

5. Where are you currently in meeting your plan?

6. What resources are needed to master your plan?

7. Write all the information from Steps 1 through 6 on a sheet of paper. It's okay to include groups, charts, or graphs. There is no right or wrong way.

8. On your completed list, identify specific tasks required to activate the list.

9. You are getting close to completing your plan. Now set a time frame for each of your tasks.

10. Create a visual timeline/flowchart/graph on paper. For each task, indicate what action is required, and set a realistic time to achieve it. Remember: while sometimes you must be flexible in planning, never lose sight of your goals. Failure to plan is planning to fail.

6

Talk-to-Do Ratio

talk-to-do ratio

noun

what you say versus what you do

Origin

1998: Mathew Knowles's vernacular

Talk is definitely cheap—for the chatterbox, anyway. There's no shortage of braggarts as well as singers in the music industry. Sometimes it seems like one big talk show, by which I mean all hype and no action. If only I had a dollar for every buzzed-about new artist who never got around to delivering a debut record! My point is that excessive yacking can be, and often is, enormously costly for anyone who buys into it when the words ultimately produce nothing more than empty promises.

Perhaps fifteen years ago, the disparity between talk and action prompted me to coin the term *talk-to-do ratio*. This phrase may sound like an intricate mathematical formula of some sort, but it isn't. While I have expanded on the definition of the talk-to-do ratio over time, it is, in fact, a very simple management efficiency tool. It just so happens to be my own gut gauge for measuring the proportion of mouthy BS to real and robust action.

What do I mean by "robust action"? Take, for example, my daughter's unprecedented decision to release her new self-titled album, *Beyoncé*, complete with fourteen songs and seventeen videos, without any advance warning whatsoever. After all, the millions of dollars' worth of prerelease marketing and advertising didn't seem to help sales of new records from Lady Gaga, Katy Perry, or Justin Timberlake. "Now people only listen to a few seconds of a song on their iPods, and they don't really invest in the whole experience," Beyoncé explained in a video posted to her Facebook page. "It's all about the single and the hype. It's so much that gets between the music and the art and the fans. I felt like, I don't want anybody to get the message, when my record is coming out. I just want this to come out when it's ready and from me to my fans." Not surprisingly, the album went platinum, selling more than a million copies worldwide in less than a week.

But it was back in 1998—around the time of the release of Destiny's Child's self-titled debut album—that I originated the talk-to-do ratio. At that point, I had been immersed in the music business for nearly a decade, managing the girls' blossoming careers. Although I knew in my heart that the group was on a trajectory toward inevitable superstardom, my frustration was at the breaking point with all the stifling hot air that the recording industry generates like the blow-dryers in a hair salon. After racking up two triumphant decades in Corporate America as a salesman—a profession in which there's a premium on talkativeness to be sure—I was absolutely stunned by the towering ratio of talk to inactivity that I witnessed in show business. Hype business is more like it!

That's not to say there weren't some salespeople who could give an incredible presentation—just talk, talk, talk from memory—without listening when the customer gave feedback. They didn't hear what was being said, so naturally, their follow-up was awful. They wouldn't have that proposal the next day as promised. All they had to offer were lame excuses. I'm sure you know some like these, and hopefully you aren't one of them.

In both Corporate America and entertainment, the problem of backing up talk with action appears to be widespread. The consequences of talking the talk without walking the walk can be devastating, not to mention disappointing. The music industry is littered with failed projects, missed opportunities, tarnished finances, and crushed careers resulting from relentless inactivity that was preceded by abundant blather. I've seen executives lose their jobs because they based decisions on talkers who didn't deliver. In the end, they couldn't talk themselves out of unemployment.

Critics frequently point to "the creative process" as the major reason for the music industry's vast imbalance between talk and action. Yet advertising, television production, and other creative businesses have an impressive history of backing up their noisemaking with concrete results. The fact of the matter is that it's a hype-fueled industry where everyone is always looking for the Next Big Thing. Not even veteran producers and legendary record-company honchos like Ahmet Ertegun, Clive Davis, LA Reid, and Donnie Ienner can absolutely guarantee that a hit single will be the end result. The magic formula remains ever elusive, as trends and tastes—not to mention technologies—change over time.

As a record label executive and manager over that period, I fell victim countless times to reassuring talk that was not supported with subsequent action. Once, for example, I scheduled a major R&B artist I represented for an appearance on one of the national morning talk shows. I planned it for weeks in advance, and the show had advertised and promoted the appearance for its millions of loyal viewers. The excited artist realized what a big opportunity this would be and talked endlessly about going on the show. Just imagine what most aspiring musicians would give to be booked on any of the network morning shows. And yet on the specific morning of the scheduled booking, the artist was nowhere to be found—a no-show, as they say. Needless to say, never again has that artist been invited back. The transgression hurt the artist's career as well as my own organization. My reputation, I suppose, also took a hit as a result.

Record-label promotion staffers were also notorious for spouting off about their ability to get a record in heavy rotation, and straight to the top of the playlist, at a particular popular radio station. More often than I care to remember, they weren't even able to—or worse still, didn't even try to—get a foot in the broadcaster's door.

For their part, producers mouthed off constantly about how it "won't be a problem" to deliver an album on time. Based on those delusions-cum-falsehoods, my label would naturally begin intense preparations, the setup for the upcoming release. All sorts of important decisions are impacted by the promise of delivering a record. For example, other potential releases aren't scheduled for that same time frame to avoid label-mate competition. In the end, however, to quote Simon and Garfunkel, there was only the sound of silence emanating from the recording studio where the long overdue album was to have been recorded. (This similarly happens in Corporate America in delivering a product to market on time.)

The frustration and, occasionally, outright damage caused by big mouths began to weigh on me. For the sake of my sanity, I had to come up with a way of assessing the great divide between verbosity and activity—and accountability. I needed a gauge that would aid me in avoiding as many windbags as possible. I needed a tool that improved my ability to ferret out the industry's successful professionals—the serious music men and women who did not rely on small talk but were capable of making big things happen. Of course these people existed at Sony; I merely needed to find them. And it was critical that I become more efficient at this task to maximize the achievements and accomplishments that I knew were possible for Destiny's Child, Beyoncé, Nas, Mario, Lyfe Jennings, Solange, Kelly Rowland, Michelle Williams, and my own career as a manager.

Out of this need emerged the talk-to-do ratio. What are the important variables that go into a gut calculation, you might ask? What are the telltale signs of talk/action imbalance? In retrospect, there's nothing mysterious about it; it mostly involves careful observation and attention to the track record of the people sitting across the desk or table from you. Equally, or perhaps more, important is to ask oneself this question: how do successful people behave?

When it comes to the talk-to-do ratio, it's all about follow-up; the lack thereof is the primary identifying marker of action-averse chatterboxes. What they do best—yack—ends up sabotaging their ability to act in several ways. Talkers constantly overcommit, rendering themselves unlikely to follow up. They can get so engrossed in their yammering that they become oblivious to the commitments flowing past their lips. They obligate themselves to do things that they don't have the expertise to deliver. For instance, A&R reps (that is, talent scouts) claim that they will give me a digital strategy for an upcoming album release. I know that's not going to happen, because they've talked themselves far beyond their zone of competency. I know a lot of people in entertainment who engage in what I like to think of as a Jedi mind trick—they just talk, talk, talk and inevitably start believing their own lies.

When I find myself struggling to get a word or two edgewise into a conversation, I am confident that the person I'm talking to has a low talk-to-do ratio. I have found myself in these circumstances many times. Even when I recognized this early in the conversation, professionalism would not allow me to abruptly walk away. But that person captured too little of my modest chatting while carelessly promising too much on his end of the conversation (his monologue, really). Naturally, because he was droning on and hardly listening, I could anticipate no, or deeply flawed, follow-up on his part.

Contrast this with the most successful people I know in the entertainment business and beyond. Their follow-up is impeccable and on point. They do exactly what they say—and often, more than they say. Typically, they have a strong team behind them to ensure thorough follow-up. Successful people then can give directives. In my case, I have an incredible assistant, Lin Almanza, who anchors my team. I know the things I'm not good at, and I ensure that Lin is great at them. Knowing your strengths and weaknesses is a helpful way to not talk yourself into commitments that are impossible to keep; it is actually a sign of strength rather than weakness. When you observe a solid team behind the person who does the talking, the probability is greater that you are interacting with someone who has a favorable talk-to-action ratio. The convergence of strong team-building skills and action-oriented abilities is yet another example of how successful people often embody many, if not most, of the ten traits in this book.

When successful people talk, it is in a clear and economical pattern. Initially, they convey context with a concise verbal snapshot of the full story—a vivid summary, if you will. This provides a broader understanding of the issue, task, or action at hand. Then they quickly zero in on the precise nature of the follow-up action required—the bottom line, in other words.

This targeted approach takes me back to my corporate training at Xerox. Management taught us a lot about netting things out and talking context. You're just not going to find that sort of training in the music business. Or, necessarily, any training at all. There's no educational requirement to work in entertainment. I have never heard anybody say that you are required to have an education—maybe for specific corporate-level management positions, marketing, accounting, and IT jobs. But educated or (as the case may be) uneducated, everyone seems to have been born with the gift of gab.

Associates have asked me whether I ever talk for the express purpose of motivating myself to action. The reasoning behind such a strategy is somewhat convoluted. It goes like this: if you babble on and on about what you will do, but then renege or don't perform, you'll be seen as a failure. The prospect of being perceived as failure, the thinking goes, becomes a powerful motivational force for following up on all of that talk.

For me, the answer is an emphatic no. I don't talk to force myself to act. Nor am I aware that it happens to be a strategy of any of the successful folks to whom you will be introduced in these pages. I find the whole concept of having to motivate myself to do the right thing baffling.

I don't have to overcommit myself to a situation in which I could lose, say, a million dollars if I don't get back to you tomorrow. That would certainly motivate me to get back to you tomorrow, but any successful person would get back to you regardless. The dollar amount would not matter. It's just professional integrity to follow up and do what you say you'll do. Successful people, if they were not able to do as they promised, would at least let you know.

So in general, I prefer to talk a little and act a lot. Trumpeting in advance, for example, that I would have multiple artists in the top ten of Billboard's gospel chart would not have inspired me to strive any harder to make it happen. At times, I struggle over this issue of talk versus action. On more than one occasion, I have been at odds with my label's publicist, whose job it is to talk to the media about what we plan to do and are already doing. I will say, "You're doing way too many advance press releases; let's just act first." But I do realize there are times when I have to do what's best for Music World because we are in a perception-driven industry where image is everything to some people.

On the other hand, I realize that trumpeting our accomplishments— after we have acted and triumphed, that is—can be extremely positive. It is a powerful strategy, for example, for wooing unsigned artists who are eager to join a label with highly motivated management. Or, perhaps even more advantageous, such talk could land in the ear of an established gospel star close to the end of a contract at a rival label. He or she may be pondering whether to stay put or possibly venture somewhere else. If that individual happens to hear about all the success at Music World, then yes, I want to be a part of that kind of conversation.

But in general, successful folks simply don't have time for idle talk. It is a waste of valuable time. On any given day, most successful people have a limited window, and they often have to accomplish a lot in that little amount of time. That's another reason they quickly talk context and then move swiftly to netting it out.

If I had to quantify my own talk-to-do ratio, I'd like to think that I am an 8.5 out of 10—talking a bit and acting a whole lot. That's because

I don't think anybody is a 10. The most successful people in the world can't function without talking. And in my role, I have to leave room for growth—to get to 9 or, ideally, 9.5.

Ambitious newcomers in the music industry flock to talent showcases, where record labels introduce emerging acts—or unsigned artists vie for a label's attention. I first met Ricky Anderson, a Houston-based entertainment lawyer, at a showcase for Destiny's Child in our hometown. It must have been a year or two before the group's debut album was released in 1998. That's because Ricky—lawyer for beloved talk-show host Steve Harvey, gospel superstar Yolanda Adams, and Oscar-winning actress Mo'Nique—represented one of the album's producers: D'wayne Wiggins, a founding member of the 1990s soul/R&B group Tony! Toni! Toné! From that point on, Ricky and I seemed to always turn up in the same place at the same time, almost always far from Houston.

Once I was attending a meeting at a restaurant on Sunset Boulevard in Los Angeles and spotted Ricky having lunch. We chatted briefly. I went my way, and he went his. The very next morning around ten o'clock, we had another chance encounter—in Manhattan. Neither of us had mentioned that we would be flying to New York the day before.

Obviously, Ricky is a very successful man of action you would do well to study and listen to carefully, especially when he is expounding on what gets him going.

Two things: I love a challenge, and I think ambition is almost contagious depending on the household where you grew up.

I am from a small town in Michigan by the name of Benton Harbor. It's like four by four square miles, so everybody knows one another. I happen to be from a single-parent home and was raised by a single mother. I had to look at picking up challenging jobs—and male role models—outside of my home. A lot of the male leaders I admired were very ambitious and thought outside the box. And they were self-motivated too. I always appreciated and respected those traits. If it was something that needed to be done, they really got it done. And they taught me to look at life in the same way—never put off till tomorrow what you can do today. Get as much done as possible every day. Use what you need to get done as a measuring barometer. Put it on your schedule.

For example, I've got this interview down on my calendar—I start here and finish there, today. Make sure I fulfill all obligations. Having a goal for perfection is important. Nobody's perfect except the Big One upstairs, but make sure that you are good at what you do and always deliver. Reliability is an important quality.

It's not only talk that is important. Listening is key. You learn a lot more from listening than from talking. Clients always leave my office with information about the range of services I can provide. So it's just as important for me to listen to what people need. Listening is critically important, as a matter of fact. Think about it: you have to listen for what a client's needs are in order to satisfy them, right? As for talking, you have to talk enough to provide a thorough understanding of what you can deliver. Then you must take action immediately to accomplish your goal.

First, communicate the concept—what we've got to accomplish, the end goal. Then move on to the action—completing the objective. That basically comes down to scheduling. You make sure that you use every second of your day as wisely as you can. In essence: get the most out of your time each and every day.

Procrastination is a character defect that I refuse to tolerate—whenever you hear someone who wants to repeat the same thing or move too slowly, that is a red flag. You can monitor from a module perspective how long it should take to get something done, particularly if it is a simple task, such as reading or writing a letter. If it takes a person two or three days to get that done, then that person is clearly distracted or the task is not an important priority. I am not saying you should prioritize your time with matters that aren't urgent. But if you put it on your checklist to get done today, it really should get done today. No excuses.

I learned a lot from my mother. She has always been a self-proclaimed busybody. She worked for thirty-two years in a factory up in Michigan. And at seventy-eight years old, she worked on President Obama's reelection campaign.

I can't think of anybody I know who does more. She is a church woman; we went to church five days a week. She was involved in everything—in our home, in our community, and of course, in our fellowship.

My illustrious career officially began at the age of twelve when I had a paper route. I did that daily, and then on weekends I would cut lawns. I also raked leaves; I cleaned rain gutters when they were clogged; in the winter, I shoveled snow. I don't remember a time when I wasn't a multitasker— obviously, I learned that from my mom. In college, I got involved in a fraternity.

Then in law school, I was class president and a vice governor for the American Bar Association, college division. I took the bar exam early and passed it while I was still taking classes in law school. I've just always been that person who wanted to be aggressive, to attack that obligation, to not be afraid of getting the job done.

These days, when I'm not working at my law firm, I lecture. Currently, I am in my fifteenth year as an adjunct at the Thurgood Marshall School of Law, teaching entertainment law. I am chairperson of the National Bar Association, which is over the entire fifty states. I'm former president of the Houston Bar Association. Like Mathew, I am a governor for the Grammys. I'm the chairperson for Houston Community College's commercial music department.

These aren't new challenges. I've been governor of the Grammys for eight years, a lecturer for nearly twice that long. I firmly believe in getting involved, because you can only keep what you have by giving back.

Does it take a lot of time and energy to stay connected and engaged? Yes. Is it worth it? Absolutely.

My wife has been putting up with me for twenty-eight years. I share parenting responsibilities for our kids: I am in my children's lives and help to keep them focused too. I run a full practice here with entertainment television, music, and film. We have ten or twelve nationally syndicated shows on television at the same time, several Grammy-winning talents that are charting on Billboard, movies with box office profits upwards of $80 million, $90 million, $100 million—all of this happening simultaneously. I have a *lot to be thankful for. But I've surrounded myself with a talented team, and we have a strong infrastructure. I'm no one-man band, and I never forget that fact.*

Here's how it works in a nutshell: select a goal, focus on it, and complete the task at hand. It is a simple process, so don't overcomplicate it. Once you know your objective for today, get it done. Prioritize it. If you have a checklist of five things, schedule your day accordingly. If each of those things takes an hour, recognize and accept that it's going to take five hours. It is a matter of monitoring your time and using every second wisely. You can put your task on a list. But if you ignore the list, then the task won't get done. You've just got to stay focused. Staying focused is the key.

I am currently working on a bunch of TV-show deals, including a few that I can't mention yet. Steve Harvey is on NBC now with a talk show. He cleared 98 percent of the country to appear on local TV stations. That's huge for him. He recently retired from stand-up comedy; we delivered that program for a pay-per-view event. I've been his lawyer for twenty years. I'm really proud of what he's done. In his younger days, he said, "I want to do a talk show." That's one of those talk-to-do moments for sure. Because he talked about doing it, and now he's actually gone and done it. It may have taken some time to get it done, but that's major.

Yolanda Adams is coming into television too. Mo'Nique has accomplished her goals, being an Academy Award winner. In short, a lot of good stuff is happening with my gals and guys. What does the future hold? Big things.

The audiences for the biggest prime-time entertainment shows are puny compared with the tens of millions or more viewers who tune in for sporting events—the NBA finals, the Super Bowl, and of course, the World Cup. For decades now, music has been an integral part of these productions. And for any artist to be featured on such a massive platform is a dream come true. Around 2004, after Destiny's Child had achieved global superstardom and Beyoncé had proven her appeal as a solo act, I was approached by one of the industry's greatest producers working today. As ABC-TV's executive producer of music events, David Saltz has masterminded Super Bowl halftime shows featuring the likes of the Rolling Stones, Paul McCartney, and Prince.

David proposed that we partner to propel Destiny's Child beyond the comparatively narrow reach of music fans and into the broader—and unparalleled—stratosphere of audiences for professional sports. And that's exactly where we traveled together. In 2004, Destiny's Child were among the pregame concert performers for *NFL Opening Kickoff*, which launched that year's football season at Foxboro stadium, home field of the then reigning Super Bowl champions, the New England Patriots. Destiny's Child went on to open NBA playoff games that were broadcast on ABC and ESPN as well.

It goes without saying that David, a true maestro of his field, has mastered the art of minimalist talk. Certainly talk is an occupational necessity for coordinating mammoth television productions. Even more, though, sports–music television is nothing if not all about action. Given the inherent excitement and adrenaline rush that comes with the territory, it's particularly interesting to know what gets David's juices surging.

The chance to do something that hasn't been done before is always exciting. You can't get sidetracked by people—lots of people—who will insist that it can't be done or it will never work. That's the easiest thing to say. But look at every great leader: you need to have conviction in your own ideas and then go about connecting dots to make them happen. It's about passion, belief, and interest in what you're trying to achieve. Also, in life, your only real possessions are your actions. So when you commit to something, you had better do it.

My first great mentor was my father. He instilled this idea that there are three types of people. You can be a person who watches things that happen, or you can be a person who wonders about what happens. But what you really need to be is the third type of person: someone who makes things happen. That sort of got drilled into me at an early age. So that has been my particular path, and it's become my mission in life. Not just talking about things, not merely wondering, not worrying about things that are beyond my control, but sincerely trying to make great things happen—spectacular things.

Another lesson I have learned over and over again in life is that in many ways it is about the company you keep. Make sure to surround yourself with positive people with the same motivation and action-oriented outlook. Negative people will just drain your energy and, ultimately, drag you down.

Then just do the best you can. Admittedly, I sometimes work on stuff that doesn't happen, despite all the effort I put into a project. Generally, you will encounter obstacles in your path; just be careful that you don't get stuck on them. You want to go around them, over them, under them—or plow right through them. The point is to get out of the problem and into the solution.

So you've got to have tenacity. That is a key character trait of action-oriented people. To paraphrase a great songwriter: if you know where you're going, any road can take you there.

I don't deny that talking is critically important in assembling the multitude of elements that go into a television production. But having been a consultant to ABC, ESPN, the NFL, and the Miami Dolphins, I know better than most the point when talking should stop. Because as the saying goes, the show must go on.

I love a dialogue that involves a genuine exchange of ideas. I love a symposium for musing about a vision. But times have changed for us as professional people, in our personal lives, and as hobbyists. We're pretty stretched to capacity. Technology has changed our lives. If you want a day off to do nothing, you have to make some effort to stick to it because there's stuff coming at you from all over the place—cell phones ringing, portable devices going off, e-mails blasting from five different accounts, a desktop full of invites to different events. There's not a lot of free time to waste these days.

You have to ascertain pretty quickly: is this an idea or project or opportunity that can lead to a result? That's something you learn as you get older. You learn to discriminate. An idea that can be executed and actually happen is something you want to spend time discussing. If it's something that will be impossible to get done, move on. Don't spend a lot of time on it or go through a long process. I think that comes from experience and years of knowing how to get things done in the most efficient manner. Then regardless of whatever field you're in, you are pretty savvy when it comes to figuring out whether something can happen or not. You tend to want to spend more time on fewer things that can happen than a lot of time on ideas that are not realistic. I am very oriented toward the former as opposed to the latter.

In 2012, I did the seventieth birthday party for Mohammed Ali in Las Vegas. That was an epic production—it was monumental. So I'm very excited that we had such a great success. Everyone turned out for it, from the worlds of sports, entertainment, and business. But we are planning more big, big ideas for subsequent years, which I promise you will be equally if not more exciting.

I also launched something unique with Mathew that was a massive success. I knew Mathew planned to release a DVD of Beyoncé's live performance at the Las Vegas Wynn Hotel in 2009. When these types of products are released, there's really only one primary sales season in mind: the holidays. And it always kicks off with that landmark day, Black Friday, the day after Thanksgiving. I told Mathew that I had a great idea to set up the DVD. I wanted to take all the footage from the Wynn event and then shoot some original stuff surrounding the show. Also, I wanted to do an original interview with Beyoncé, telling the story of how the whole show came together. I wanted to run it as a broadcast special on ABC on Thanksgiving night. He said, "Boy, would that be great, because I don't think anyone has ever done a record release the day after you do a TV special. I don't believe that people won't buy something if they've already seen it on TV. I believe more people will buy it." This was proven with the success of American Idol *and, later,* The Voice. *The biggest visibility is on television. He said, "If you're going to secure a broadcast, then we are going to make it work."*

It was so successful the first year that we did it a second time in 2010 when Mathew released a DVD of Beyoncé's world tour on Black Friday. We made magic two years in row, which was really unprecedented. No one has ever done back-to-back Thanksgiving night specials. And I believe that on both nights, we managed to set a ratings record.

ICM agent Dennis Ashley stalked me by land and, most impressively, by air. Ashley—a major force in urban music who has represented Mary J. Blige, Ne-Yo, and Chris Brown—went far out of his way in order to seal a deal to represent Destiny's Child back in the late 1990s. And, man, am I thankful. Had Dennis, who was actually with Creative Artists Agency (CAA) at the time, been any less determined to do business with me, I might never have met his remarkable colleague, the film agent Andrea Nelson Meigs, who guides Beyoncé's movie career to this day.

Around 1998, when "No, No, No" became Destiny's Child's breakthrough hit, I was on a business trip to Los Angeles. Not surprisingly, Dennis, who is based there, turned up with yet another turbocharged pitch. *What part of no don't you understand?* I thought to myself. In hopes of escaping him, I mentioned that I was rushing to hop a flight to Virginia, where the girls would be performing. As I settled into my seat for the cross-country flight, I heard someone say my name (to quote another beloved Destiny's Child hit). Lo and behold, it was Dennis, who was positioned on the aisle directly opposite me. By the time the flight landed, he had persuaded me to sign on the dotted line.

Once we were on CAA's client roster, we were introduced around the Beverly Hills headquarters. That's when we met Andrea, who was a newly minted agent back then. I was extremely impressed. She was young, extremely smart, and had impressive credentials. I was surprised to learn that she had abandoned her first career as a lawyer in the mid-1990s to break into the talent-agency business by going to work for CAA—in the mailroom, no less. She was only the second African American woman to work her way up the corporate ladder at CAA.

If those attributes weren't attractive enough, Andrea was beginning to carve out a niche in the entertainment business, representing artists who aspired to extend their talents into other areas of the industry. Although she would later represent A-list Oscar winners like Halle Berry, the work that stood out most to me was her representation of Cedric the Entertainer, whose career she had elevated from television to the big screen. It reflected exactly the kind of action orientation that would propel Beyoncé's own career beyond recording studios and onto Hollywood film sets.

I certainly don't mind when other people describe me as an action-oriented agent, but I would never talk about myself that way. What I like to say instead is that I keep my word. If that translates into being an action-oriented person, then so be it. But again, the way I look at it is: I like to keep my word. When I say I'm going to do something at ICM, you had better believe that I'll do it.

I have been a very self-motivated person and an initiator since I was a child. As an adult, this is something that I am kind of surprised about now as I reflect back on my childhood. But I still remember it vividly. I was probably eight or nine years old at the time, and I recall keeping an index box as opposed to, say, a toy box. Inside the box was a collection of different cards with my handwritten goals on them. And if you can believe it, I even had the cards divided up into sections: my immediate goals, my short-term goals, then a five-year section and, yes, a ten-year section. I've always been a checklist type of person. I like to check off goals—you know, "mission accomplished," "goal completed," and "task finished." I've just always been like that.

That mind-set has spilled over not only into my personal life, being a mother of four children, but also into my professional life and what I do on a day-to-day basis in representing clients. I meet with each of them at the top of the year, and we set specific goals. Whenever I sign a new client, we meet to discuss past goals and what the goals should be for the future—immediate, short-term, and long-term goals. And then we devise a realistic strategy. Later on, we may need to make minor adjustments to the goals and strategies. Think of it as fine-tuning a career trajectory.

As far as influences are concerned, I would say that my father is very much like me. Or rather, I am just like my father. Whether it is genetic, hereditary, or just by osmosis, I learned pretty much everything from that man. He is the type of person who when he says he's going to do something, he does it. Not keeping your word is never acceptable. He's seventy-six years old now, and he's still helping me out with transporting my kids to their after-school activities. After a visit to the doctor's office the other day, he needed crutches to get around with a brace on his foot. But of course he insisted on picking up my daughter, regardless. He's so much about, "If I tell you I'm going to do something, then I am going to do it." That's pretty much been instilled in me from when I was a child—that kind of do-what-you-say-you're-going-to-do-or-else attitude.

Has there ever been a time when I wasn't so action-oriented? The only time that may have come into play was in my later adult life, when my second daughter got really sick and had to be hospitalized. We ultimately lost her; she passed away. I realized at that point that no matter how much I did, no matter what my goals were, it was not ultimately in my control. It was a part of God's plan that I had to accept. That was the first time I realized that I cannot control every aspect of my life—or the lives of my children—completely, no matter how hard I try.

As a result, I now have a different outlook on life. I will do everything I can to accomplish my goals, but at a certain given point, I do have to turn it over to God. Therefore, I pray only for knowledge of God's will for me and the strength to carry it out.

Over the years, I've had to teach myself to do more talking, particularly in this business. In Hollywood, there's a lot of talking that goes on, as you can imagine—it's almost like a form of currency. So I will sit in a meeting or on a conference call, and there will be a back-and-forth conversation regarding positioning. I often find that I am the one who is ready to get off the call quickly. I am done talking, and that's precisely because I am ready to execute the plan. I'm most likely going to be the first person to initiate and schedule the all-important follow-up meeting. And that meeting is to go over what has been accomplished since the initial conversation.

To be honest, I have had to teach myself to slow it down a bit, to have more patience and discussion and give people the opportunity to state their position—and justify their position in light of the bigger goal. Not that it necessarily changes what my overall objective is, but there is, particularly in this business, definitely an intention or a desire to have a conversation before you get down to the meat-and-potatoes of a negotiation. That's something I have really had to push myself to incorporate into my own personal style of doing business.

There is a lot of hollow talk in this town: "Let's do lunch," "I'll have my people call your people," etc. But for me, if I tell someone that I am going to call and set up a lunch, I really do call and schedule a lunch at my earliest convenience. If I tell you I am going to get scripts and materials over to you, trust me: I'm going to get it done. If it's not done that same day, then it has to be done within two days maximum. And I'm looking for the same type of treatment and respect in return. When someone says that they are going to set up something, did they do it? Is there a prompt follow-up? To me, that is the biggest sign of an action-oriented person—there is an immediate follow-up plan in the works.

I represent Salim Akil and Mara Brock Akil, among many others. They are the writer-producer-director team behind the remake of Sparkle, *which turned out to be Whitney Houston's final movie. These clients were primarily working in television at the beginning of their careers. A couple of years ago, they said, "We'd really like to get in the motion-picture business." So we set that goal. Now* Sparkle *is their second movie. Mara has written and Salim has directed. As far as the next action point, we're working on getting the third one done. There are a handful of other clients who are looking to take their work to the next level—to the critical level—by which I mean getting the critical awareness and award recognition. So that's an ongoing goal with several of my clients, Beyoncé included.*

Quiz: Talk-to-Do Ratio

On a scale of 1 to 10—with 1 being the lowest and 10 being the highest—let's find out how you measure up when it comes to being proactive versus procrastinating.

1. In general, how would you rate your own ability to follow up and honor your commitments? Write down that number.

2. When you make commitments to others, how consistent are you in fulfilling those obligations? Write down that number.

3. How timely are you with your follow-up and fulfillment of commitments? Write down that number.

   Add those three numbers together. If the total is 23 or greater, then congratulations! You are more about doing than talking, and you may now move on to the next chapter. However, if you scored less than 23, let's examine why. Please answer the following questions:

4. What are some issues that frequently get in the way of honoring your commitments in a timely manner? Write them down. For example, you may find that you are not well organized and therefore are easily distracted. Or you may have a habit of overcommitting yourself. You may even hesitate to begin a new task simply because you have a fear of failure.

5. Look at your answers. Why do you think that these issues consistently arise?

6. Can you think of some ways to avoid these issues in the future and to improve your follow-up overall? Write down your ideas.

7. Carefully review your answers to the last three questions. Do not be surprised if you detect some small degree of narcissism or self-absorption. Do you think you have a habit of making excuses to explain your poor talk-to-do ratio?

8. Now, what are you willing to do in order to change your behavior? Write down some suggestions for self-improvement—and commit to them!

7

Risk Taking

risk

noun

a situation involving exposure to danger

verb

expose (someone or something valued) to harm or loss

Origin

mid-17th century: from French *risque* (noun), *risquer* (verb); from Italian *risco* "danger" and *rischiare* "run into danger"

Almost daily, I interact with people who proudly proclaim themselves to be fearless takers of risks. Typically, they announce this with great braggadocio, as if risk taking is the ultimate testosterone-charged fuel for big business. I wonder, do they know what that word actually means? After all, that used to be my modus operandi too. On more occasions than I care to recall, I have casually described myself as a risk taker. But many actions that I once considered risky were, in hindsight, not so much. In most cases, as it turned out, my actions were not the infatuations with peril that I had romanticized them to be. More often than not, I had merely embraced a chance to achieve success after weighing my decision with calculated precision.

In retrospect, certainly the earliest—and one of the biggest—of my presumed "risky" decisions was hardly a dangerous move at all. But it was a literal move: in December of 1976, I relocated from Nashville to my current hometown of Houston, arriving with little more than a sofa to sleep on (as a welcome gesture, an old fraternity brother had generously agreed to put me up for a month). I had visited Houston only once before—to watch Tennessee State University thrash Texas Southern University—but it was evidently love at first sight. Not that my business prospects were grim in Nashville. As a matter of fact, my career was on a solid path at AT&T, where I had worked for the two years since graduating from nearby Fisk University in 1974.

Houston just seemed to call out for me to make the city my home. As far as my eyes could see, there were career opportunities that didn't even exist in Nashville in the mid-1970s. What I did not fully understand to the extent that I do now is that the era of affirmative action had recently dawned in Houston, and career prospects could not have been brighter for minorities.

Sure enough, during my first two weeks in my new hometown, I landed not one but two jobs—at Lanier Business Products and Pitney Bowes, both office-equipment companies. For one week, I worked at both simultaneously (a risky move in my mind) before finally choosing Pitney Bowes. I have never regretted that decision.

Today, I ask myself: What risk did I expose myself to in moving to Houston? Was there really any possibility of relentless and hopeless unemployment? Was I truly concerned about the source of my next meal and whether or not I would have a roof over my head for long? Honestly, no. After all, behind my urge to relocate to Houston in the first place was the city's vast array of untapped career opportunities.

Risk, I have concluded over the years, is easily one of the most misunderstood and complex concepts in your professional life—or, for that matter, life in general. The word dates back to circa 1661, while the origin of the idea can be traced to the philosophers of ancient Greece. These days, risk has nuanced meanings across a broad range of fields and disciplines, from finance and insurance to health and even the environment.

To psychologists, sociologists, mathematicians, and theorists of every stripe, risk is a concept worthy of endless study. Devouring the multitude of books on this topic could chew up a good chunk of a lifetime. Consider a few popular and prominent titles: *Risk and Other Four-Letter Words; Risk: The Science and Politics of Fear;* and *The Book of Risks.* In the world of financial investing, risk overshadows everything. One publishing company, the aptly named Risk Books, has carved out a niche in the category, promoting itself as "a world leader in specialist books on risk management and the financial markets."

For me personally, risk simply implies that I might fail at a given endeavor. Despite the potential for failure, I choose to have faith and proceed anyway, because the worth or value of a successful outcome greatly exceeds the fallout involved with coming up short. In other words, the upside of victory outweighs the downside of defeat. My interactions with successful people lead me to believe that most share my straightforward and practical take on risk taking.

In 1988 it was clear to me that a shift was happening at Xerox that could mean the medical division would merge with another division of Xerox internally or close completely. Seeing the writing on the wall, I became proactive and got a head hunter to scour the marketplace for sales and marketing opportunities in diagnostic images. As fate would have it, the former president of Xerox Medical Systems had left a year earlier and became president of one of the top five diagnostic imaging companies, Picker International. Mind you, it helps when you were the number-one sales rep, so needless to say when this sales and marketing position became available, I got the job. My position was sales specialist for MRI and CT scanners.

What was the risk? In 1988 very few blacks worked in pharmaceutical, medical devices and instruments, and diagnostic imaging. Certainly I can't with certainty say that I was the only black to sell diagnostic imaging equipment, but I can say with certainty that I was among the very few who did. To this day I've yet to meet anyone of color who sells MRI/CT scanners.

Picker International was behind the pack of GE, Siemens, Phillips, and Toshiba in the sale of CT/MRI. Today Picker has merged with Phillips. Although I had a six-figure guarantee, being one of the first with a company that wasn't the market leader was a significant risk. I remember my first sales call to MD Anderson Radiology Department in Houston, Texas. MD Anderson was noted then, and still today, as one of the top cancer research centers that often is ranked number one. So getting a sale at MD Anderson not only positioned your product as an industry leader but certainly gave you huge bragging rights in the diagnostic sales arena. I remember calling on then chairman of the department Dr. Sidney Wallace, who was a delightful Jewish gentleman. I had been trained at Xerox always "top down selling" and starting at the very top of an organization. Dr. Wallace's assistant was equally as warm as Dr. Wallace. After all, we normally hire in our own image. I explained who I was and gave my pitch: "I am a new sales rep assigned to MD Anderson, and I only want Dr. Wallace to put name to face when I call in the future." Like most sales reps, I only needed two minutes of his time, always hoping an opportunity would come out of those precious minutes. Dr. Wallace's assistant was reluctant at first, yet I since saw in her eyes a willingness to help. She actually shared to me later that there had never been an African American to call on the Radiology Department of MD Anderson. After giving her my card she came back from Dr. Wallace with, "He will see you now." When I walked through his door, he screamed, "You're not Jewish!" (I have only one *t* in Mathew), and I responded, "Hell yes I am."

Sometimes there are just moments that connect people and allow you to use your ability to seize the moment and take that risk of hearing no! I built an incredible relationship with Dr. Wallace and his staff over the years and successfully sold over six million dollars in sales.

So why do I no longer see myself as a taker of sizeable risks? Studying my past experiences and achievements, I now realize that my so-called risk taking in most instances involved little or no chance of ending in defeat. I always managed to control the risk—by observing that the Houston job market was increasingly vibrant at the time of my move, for instance. At heart, I have always been a careful decision maker rather than a reckless risk taker.

I often cite Kobe Bryant as the perfect example of what I like to call "empty risks." With the clock ticking down and the game on the line, he's the guy who will want to take the last shot every time. Of course, the result could be that he misses the basket completely. Every basketball fan recognizes Kobe's risk in taking the shot. Not Kobe, however—he has mentally as well as physically prepared himself for that particular moment. He has practiced, practiced, and practiced some more. He has visualized a successful outcome in his mind: a game-winning shot, with no time remaining on the clock.

To focus excessively on risk can sometimes be so paralyzing that the window for seizing an opportunity is at, yes, risk. I, for one, should know. I have allowed more than one golden moment to pass by that could have resulted in an extraordinarily enriching payday. Like the time back in 2011 when a stock promoter phoned to pitch me on buying the high-flying shares of Apple Inc. Convinced that the stock would rise even higher, he proposed that I invest $1 million in shares of the computer and digital-gadgets giant.

And I was so close to doing it. This close! Then Steve Jobs, Apple's visionary chief executive officer, lost his long battle with pancreatic cancer. I began calling various investment advisors to assess whether or not his death would impact the stock's future success. Some believed that the Apple stock would be depressed for a long, long time to come. Others expected it to rebound soon—and strongly at that. I ended up doing nothing, and then later I watched the stock soar. The point is that I wasn't about to make that investment without first consulting the opinions of insiders and industry experts. I don't believe in betting a million dollars and treating the stock market like the rich man's roulette table.

Nonetheless, this encounter reaffirmed a lesson about risk that I have come to believe in: success often results from not playing it safe. That doesn't mean I'm careless with my savings. Planning and teamwork can help minimize risk significantly, in my experience. I always assign the proper people in my organization to analyze and evaluate the potential for failure. Then they brainstorm everything that could possibly go wrong—as opposed to right—and we adjust our plan accordingly. We also come up with a backup plan—or, preferably, two. So if plan B flops, there is always plan C. I am a firm believer in devising an advance solution to any problem that may pop up along the way (or at the last minute, as is often the case in the entertainment industry).

Three of the most successful businessmen with whom I've had the pleasure of working have the same game plan when it comes to tackling big risks: For one, it's all about self-reliance. For the next, it comes down to a higher power. And the third? He wisely listens to his gut. Paxton Baker was a risk taker in everyone's eyes, with the possible exception of his boss, Bob Johnson, the billionaire founder of Black Entertainment Television (BET). That was the rap on Paxton when he and I first met in 1999, anyway. As the newly minted president of BET's upstart cable-channel offshoot, BET Jazz, he was, to quote Paxton, "pushing a snowball up a hill, professionally speaking." The entertainment world was overrun with naysayers who insisted that he had ventured beyond risk taking into recklessness—and likely financial ruin—with his leadership role at BET Jazz (now known as Centric). Jazz was a rapidly declining genre of music, they argued, and long past its hipster heyday. But Paxton, who solicited my support, had a secret risk-repellent: his mojo.

I had to believe in myself. I had to get the ball and take some shots at the basket, you know? I never go into anything believing that I can't pull it off—that's just setting yourself up for failure. I already owned a production company, PKB Arts & Entertainment, which produced music festivals, most famously the St. Lucia Jazz Festival. In 1992, BET picked up coverage of the festival. Flash forward several years to 1999. I helped Bob Johnson launch BET Jazz. I took it over with the agreement that I'd keep my business on the side. It was losing a lot of money when I started. But within three years, we broke even and reached a profit in the fourth. I sold my company to BET in 2000, just before Viacom bought it. Fortunately, with teamwork, we were able to turn it around. It has been in a growth cycle for the past few years, rising in ratings, revenue, and distribution.

You absolutely must get some breaks to succeed in this business. But breaks are something that you can actually create for yourself with a positive mental attitude and a willingness to share your blessings. Giving back happens to strengthen my self-confidence. Literally thinking that I have enough bounty to share with others develops and promotes self-confidence. I owned 100 percent of my company. But when I sold it to BET, I decided to give a piece back to the people who helped build it. After all, they came with me after the sale to assist with the launch BET Jazz. And obviously, when you are willing to share the wealth, people realize that you are a fair person who has their best interests at heart.

One of the greatest blessings? All the relationships I have built over the years. I have an open mind, a positive mental attitude, and a willingness to listen to other people. Sure enough, I found that my reputation began to precede me, so I no longer had to constantly sell myself. I eventually became known as someone who has a knack for coming up with a win-win situation and helps create the breaks that are necessary to succeed despite the risks.

Not that every risk is worth taking a chance on. Not every opportunity to win has a gold medal waiting for you at the finish line—that's just not realistic in business. The key is to look at what success could mean. For example, I'm about to embark on building a comedy awards show— the ESPYs of stand-up, sort of. Comedy is growing all the time in the entertainment industry. And there's not a comedy awards show for the urban market—yet. What is the possible return, I ask myself? If successful, what could such a show yield for our overall business? One thing is certain: if we don't take a risk, we will never find out the (perhaps profitable) answers to those questions.

After almost three decades, the Stellar Gospel Music Awards is to enthusiasts of that most uplifting and soul-stirring of genres—particularly African American audiences—what the Grammys are to fans of popular music and rock and roll. Not surprisingly, Don Jackson found a loving home for the show in the predominantly African American city of Atlanta, where his Central City Productions mounted the ceremony for many years to widespread acclaim and adoration. Until 2005, that is, when Don decided to shake things up with a risky move to my home turf of Houston for the twentieth annual event.

That is when and how I met Don, who had reached out to me at the behest of the city's mayor. I was thrilled that he had relocated the show to Houston, as it was reminiscent of my own move some two decades earlier. Almost forty years later now, I'm a Houstonian through and through. Don, however, lasted for one year and one awards show—and only then, as he will enthusiastically tell you, by the grace of God. As it was, the repercussions of Hurricane Katrina sent him packing—Houston offered shelter to Katrina refugees from New Orleans in the Convention Center the following year. Mother Nature simply imposed a risk that was too great for Don to take on again, despite his steadfast belief in divine intervention and assistance.

I believe a risk is worth taking as soon as an idea comes to mind. Because I also believe that all good ideas come directly from God. I am a faith-based person, and so I try to follow a spiritual path—and the God within me— and not question or doubt myself. The faith I have in God-given ideas will be surrounded with all that is needed for any risk to be successful. I take that approach in everything I do. As long as I put forth the time and effort to do the right thing—and continue to have faith in God's nurturing love—I know I'll be fine.

Gospel superstar Yolanda Adams is from Houston, and of course she was a big part of the Stellar Awards. Not surprisingly, we had been approached by a number of different cities. The idea was to expose the taping of the awards to other areas with a sizable African American demographic. At the time, Houston had a black mayor. That inspired my decision to step out of our longtime comfort zone of Atlanta. But it sure took a lot to do that.

I remember that we visited various venues in Houston that were supposed to be available to us. But in the end, the only place they could put us was the Convention Center—on the third level, with no stage, no seats, and a concrete floor! My director came back and said we should seriously rethink this move: "Let's just go back to Atlanta, where we know what to expect from our venue, such as seats and a stage, for starters." But I said no. With God's help we could make it work. That meant we had to construct a stage from scratch and import bleachers. All the effort proved to be worthwhile in the end. The turnout was the biggest we've ever had for the awards. It was a unique experience, to say the least. Or rather, as I prefer to see it, a minor miracle.

Never say never, but I have no plans to do the Stellar Awards in a convention center again. We did what we had to do to make it work because Houston was so excited about the opportunity to be home to the ceremony. But only by the grace of God were we able to pull it off without a hitch.

Now that was hardly my first big risk in this business. I started my company forty-two years ago. At the time, I was working as a sales manager for a radio station in Chicago and had the desire to become an entrepreneur. My wife was pregnant with our second child. The radio station presented me with a chance to start my business on the side. They offered to look the other way in terms of my moonlighting as long as I'd continue to head the radio sales force. When I told my wife, she said, "If you're running their sales team, how much time will that give you to start your own business?" I realized that she was absolutely right—and fearless. I went back the next day and said, "Sorry, I quit. Just please pay me maternity benefits for my wife." So my first serious risk was to start my company in the first place!

God immediately surrounded me with all the love, support, and clients I needed to pay the bills. My business was marketing and advertising consulting to the African American market, but initially I hadn't known where the revenue would come from. When I told my clients at the radio station that I was leaving, they asked to become personal clients of mine. I swiftly picked up three clients to start and consequently never encountered cash-flow problems. The risk I took was leaving a very well-paying job when my wife was expecting and not knowing what the future held. But because I chose to have faith instead of living in fear and took action, God provided me with everything I needed to be successful.

Risk is something that God can manage for you, and it's important to distinguish that from careless recklessness. In my experience, every time you move forward with a positive idea, as long as you do the legitimate footwork that's inevitably involved, God will provide everything you need for that risk to pay off. So whenever ideas come to me, I'm inclined to take a chance on them. Don't get me wrong; I'll do my homework. And then I will take the risk. I don't waste any time or energy measuring the risk and pondering how much I may have to lose in the process.

Ultimately, you have to love the thrill that comes from seeing a risk you have taken slowly advance toward success. You must have passion for what you are doing and a sense of excitement from seeing it all come together. You've got be fearless—like my inspiring wife—and not be afraid of all the things that might go wrong after you take the leap. Sure, you'll come across plenty of people who will tell you why you shouldn't dare risk it and that you're crazy for leaving a safe job.

Often, we crave instant gratification and want things to happen in a certain way—and right away. What I've learned is that things don't necessarily work out in my time. But in God's time, things always work out according to His plan. So I have learned to be patient and to not beat myself up while I am waiting for the results. I just have to work harder at succeeding instead of wasting my energy on doubting the idea. If, like me, you believe that every idea is God-given—and therefore divine—then you don't doubt it or your own infinite capacity for success. Can I get an amen?

It's likely that Alex López Negrete and I would have never met if we had to rely on bumping into each other in the wide aisles in one of the many Walmart stores in Houston. Instead, our friendship began through our common good fortune in the business suites of Walmart's headquarters in Bentonville, Arkansas. To cultivate the nation's exploding Hispanic consumer base, the world's largest retailer bet on the savvy of Houston-based Lopez Negrete Communications, Alex's advertising agency. That was in 1995, a decade before Walmart and Beyoncé hitched their brands to a mutually beneficial endorsement deal. And not surprisingly, we immediately saw eye to eye. Since then, Lopez Negrete Communications—which Alex launched in 1985 with his wife, Cathy—has secured a position as one of the largest Latino-owned agencies partly because of its massive Walmart account.

Walmart became an important factor in Beyoncé's record sales at the same time as her endorsement paid robust dividends at the retailer's cash registers. Alex and I later bonded in the music arena when Houston had the opportunity to host the Latin Grammy Awards in 2008. Risk—and specifically risk-management—has been a recurring topic of our conversations throughout the years. No one has mastered the art of risk taking like Alex. Except, perhaps, for Alex's wife.

Coming to this country was the biggest risk I have ever taken. Granted, I was born in the United States, but I was raised in Mexico City. I always knew I needed to come back to America eventually to forge my own future. So I left home—and my entire family—in Mexico to travel here and work my way through college.

I met my wife the first day I arrived: June 21, 1978. Before I knew it, I was living in Texas and had applied to college, all without ever telling my parents. All of a sudden, it seems, there I was walking across a scorching hot parking lot at the University of Houston in 112 degree weather. Needless to say, had I not taken that particular risk, my life would be very, very different today. Ditto for my bank account.

Comparatively, starting a business with my wife was not such a risky venture. Many people choose to work for many years until they feel like they finally have enough experience to set out on their own and open a firm. However, I chose to not wait. My thinking was that by starting out close to the bottom, I didn't have very far to fall in the first place. At that time, my needs from an economic perspective were relatively small. But certain things started lining up for me, not the least of which was my marriage. And I have never been shy on courage or lacked the willingness to work hard. So by 1985, less than a decade after I had returned to this country, I was confident that I had the basic skill set required to launch—and run—a business.

While I realized that there were still a lot of things I obviously didn't know, I believed that I would learn on the job and figure all that out in due time along the way. For one thing, I made sure that I shut up and listened to wiser, more experienced people whenever they crossed my path. Then I tore off the rearview mirror and never looked back. Rearview mirrors are annoying things, in my view. They aren't really good for much. Most people have car accidents when they are busy looking in the rearview mirror—after all, you can't see the road ahead of you, let alone what is right in front of you, if you are always focusing on the past.

And yet, there is a thin line between calculated risk taking and self-destructive recklessness. I often ask myself: when is a risk too big to take? And the answer is simple: whenever the outcome is unclear and the risk puts too many other people in jeopardy. If there's a chance of hurting other people, a risk is clearly too big to take. Secondly, part of the science of risk taking is figuring out an accurate assessment of what the likely outcome will be—you have to weigh the various pros and cons and carefully calculate your desired outcome. The big mistake a lot of people make when they are just starting out? They take risks without even knowing what they ultimately want in terms of the end result. And I think you have to be able to differentiate short-term goals from long-term results. Strategic risks should only be taken after that crucial assessment is done.

If you do the math right, then you mitigate the potential risk substantially. Blind risk is the definition of reckless behavior, in other words. But another word of caution: when it comes to assessing risk, don't factor your gut out of the equation. A lot of people go through an intellectual evaluation process and make the mistake of ignoring their instincts altogether. You can't rely on the brain alone to properly assess a risk. That is how the margin of error can increase, exponentially. Remember: if a risk doesn't feel like a risk—which only your gut can tell you—then you are engaged in a decision-making, not a risk-taking, process. In other words, a risk that is overly calculated is no longer a risk but rather a decision.

Most successful entrepreneurs will agree that your gut will serve you well. Think of it as your own personal built-in GPS. When you ignore your gut, you are more likely to get lost, and you might even get in a bad accident while trying to find your way.

But allow me to offer more guidance when it comes to assessing risk. Again, the first step is figuring out your desired outcome—what is it that you want? An entrepreneur contemplating a risk must decide, for example, whether he or she is trying to effect a specific change. Will the outcome change if you've been doing business for a certain number of years and your financial model seems stuck in gear? Or if the model isn't doing as well as you expected—or as well as it used to do? Or if you are trying to shake things up? Are you simply bored with the old model? In general, we entrepreneurs seem to get bored pretty easily.

Without doing the desired-outcome exercise, there is no way that you can start making decisions about whether or not to take a risk. When people fail to take this extra step, it hinders their vision—they can't see beyond the short-term results. But the best and most exciting risks are the long-term plays, not the immediate gains. So ask yourself: does the risky activity have the potential to be a game changer? Is it something that might take your business to the next level? You have to dare to design your risk. Think big. Always.

Aspiring risk takers must be careful not to overanalyze. And although the best risk takers never abandon their gut feeling, they realize that their GPS only works well when it has good input—meaning the lessons learned from prior experiences. I see people who take risks throughout their careers without retaining any of the invaluable lessons learned along the way. You have to know what it feels like to fall down and skin your knee; never forget that pain. Otherwise, you're not going to do a very good job of calculating future risk. Don't forget that going with your gut does not mean going blind. I always rely on a good dash of intuition and my gut, but I also keep in mind the desired outcome I am hoping to achieve—the big picture.

Every time I take a risk that doesn't pan out, there is an invaluable lesson to be learned from failure. Walmart calls this kind of postmortem a "correction of errors," something that began with Sam Walton, the founder, back in 1962. Walmart performs a correction of errors on every risk it takes, successful or not. I realize that the name of this phrase may sound a little ominous because it implies that something failed or at least went wrong. Yet even if you were successful, it's about trying to identify things you could do differently the next time—or rather, things that can be improved upon the next time Walmart is faced with a similarly risky situation. What new data do you download into your gut? Just remember: your gut is a combination of all your previous experiences, positive as well as negative.

The gutsiest risk taker I know happens to be my wife. We have been partners in this business for twenty-seven years, and we've been married for thirty-one years. Some of the biggest risks you take in business have roots in a personal relationship. The fact that Cathy took a chance on a skinny, straggly-haired, long-bearded kid from Mexico? That was one humongous risk. Because we are business as well as romantic partners, I know for a fact that she's blessed with very strong intuition. She also tends to assume positive outcomes—that's just her nature. She always examines the risk factor just like I do. But really, she focuses on positive outcomes. And I may sound like an old hippie here, but her positive karma affects everything we do together, whereas pessimism breeds like a bad fungus.

I will be the first to admit that Cathy has helped me make the riskiest decisions of all. The building that houses our business is one such example. We own it. It is a Latino-owned medium-to-small ad agency. Seven years ago, when we ultimately decided to buy the business—a big building in Houston—she simply said, "Alex, it's time. We are going to need the space. Let's not rent; let's buy it." A serious and sizable risk, to be sure, but in the long run one of the best decisions we have ever made as a couple. There are many more examples, of course. She's a very, very ballsy chick. Her GPS is as good as anybody's I have ever seen. I've learned a lot just by being her partner and her husband. As you can see, getting married is a risk that has paid off for both of us big-time.

Quiz: Risk Taking

1. I always think of risk as the chance that something will go awry. With that in mind, do you consider yourself to be a risk taker? Why or why not?

2. If you do consider yourself to be a risk taker, why do you take risks? If you don't, why do you avoid taking risks?

3. Write down some examples of risks—big or small—you have taken in the past.

4. Were your risks worth the end results? Why or why not?

5. What do you find challenging about the concept of taking risks?

6. Innovation, risk taking, and success go hand in hand, in my opinion. List a few areas of your professional life where you could stand to take more risks.

8

Learning from Failure

failure

noun

lack of success

the omission of expected or required action

Origin

mid-17th century (originally as *failer,* in the senses "nonoccurrence" and "cessation of supply"): from Anglo-Norman French *failer* for Old French *faillir.*

I will always be haunted by my professional—and personal—failures as a businessman as well as a human being. But in retrospect, I am a better person today precisely because of my mistakes, especially the whoppers. And I am not alone: had medical researchers given up after failing to find a cure for AIDS, would the scientific community have discovered the antiviral cocktails that prevent millions of people from dying of HIV? Had it not been for the initial failure of the Wright brothers, would we have the 787s of today? Had it not been for Michael Jordan's failure to make the varsity team, would the sports world have been blessed with the greatest basketball player of all time? I am sure that dozens of Olympic athletes who took home gold medals from Sochi can also relate to the idea of learning from failure. One is not born but rather becomes a winner. My message is simple: don't give up! You never know, you just might help change the world someday. In his book *Assassination of Human Potential* Oscar J. Underwood, PhD, and his beloved brother say mistakes are reasons to grow, not reasons to quit. Growth is not a one-time event. It is progressive and ongoing. One factor that enhances and stimulates new growth is the manner in which one responds to failure.

One of my own epic missteps left Beyoncé with a blemish on her previously pristine image. On New Year's Eve in 2009, she performed at a private party on the island of St. Barths, where international jet-setters spend the holiday season.

Beyoncé was hardly the only A-lister in attendance. Guests included Jay Z, Jon Bon Jovi, Russell Simmons, LA Reid, supermodel Miranda Kerr, and BET founder Bob Johnson—the crème de la crème of moguls, models, and musicians. (The countdown to midnight was delivered by none other than Usher.) The gig, which paid $1 million–plus for a handful of songs, reflected the top tier of the entertainment market, which caters exclusively to the super-rich. Mariah Carey had entertained at the gathering the previous year. It was an easy payday and the perfect opportunity to be in a beautiful location: the famed Nikki Beach club. What could go wrong?

Well, a couple of days into 2010, a writer phoned from an obscure news website, wanting to know if Beyoncé had performed at the annual New Year's Eve bash of the Qaddafi family. Just the usual tabloid nonsense that comes with stardom, I initially assumed. But as it turned out, 2010 began on an unflattering note for us. I had dealt with a third-party promoter who was eventually linked to the family of (now deceased) Colonel Muammar el-Qaddafi, the Libyan leader who, by reputation, was a notorious tyrant and international terrorist. Tweeted photos of Beyoncé singing and dancing at the party soon went viral.

Associating Beyoncé and all that she had come to represent with a ruthless dictator could have been devastating—and quite possibly irreparable—to her otherwise flawless reputation. Naturally, we quickly renounced the Qaddafi money. Beyoncé donated her $1 million to Haiti relief efforts shortly after the January 12, 2010, earthquake there.

I, for one, never made that mistake again. And just to clarify: Beyoncé had absolutely nothing to do with that mess in the first place. I was not diligent enough as her manager, plain and simple. Our agency at the time brought the booking to us, identifying the promoter as a corporation. I never thought to inquire about who owned that private company—who might be hiding behind the corporate veil. Why am I better off because of the failure? From that headline-making screwup, I salvaged a lifelong (and invaluable) lesson in proper due diligence. From that day forward, no stone goes unturned in determining with whom I am doing business.

This is just one of the ways in which failure—or rather, fear of failure—can be a powerful motivator in one's professional life. Pick your own definition of failure. In my eyes, it's when the objective that I set out to achieve is not the end result. By that measure, I have compiled my fair share of errors and mistakes over the years. Every situation is different, and the lesson that I have learned from each experience is similarly unique. But in every case, I have internalized the resulting information about what went wrong and why. So today, whether my work day runs eight, twelve, or sixteen hours long, I always take time out to review my past setbacks in business. In fact, on any given day at the office, at least half the decisions I make are informed by those hard-earned lessons.

I have come to believe it is best to openly embrace failure rather than try to hide it or deny it. I have found that people who have achieved a certain degree of success are equally forthcoming about the times they came up short in business. No one prides himself on falling flat, of course. But if and when it happens, failure has proven to be a godsend in the careers of many people who have hit it big in the long run. And they tend to willingly share the wisdom they gained from faltering, especially with others who may benefit from it.

For years, I encouraged my artists to never discuss their private lives in interviews; those types of invasive questions were off-limits as a general rule. I used to believe that our professional life is our public life and our personal life is strictly private. I always thought we needed to keep them separate, but now I have to own my mistakes. Admittedly, it was not until my most current, highly publicized failures—of which I will not go into sordid detail—that I learned the impact our personal lives inevitably have on our professional lives. This has taken me a long time to understand; however, I have come to realize that it is absolutely impossible to separate the two when one is in any type of leadership role because the public's perception is based on our overall integrity—personal as well as professional. You have to live both congruently; social media and cameras make it impossible to hide anything these days.

Granted, sometimes people in the public eye are reluctant to acknowledge failure—Tiger Woods and Donald Sterling come to mind. On a personal note, I admit that I have failed as a husband as well as a father, which I cannot change today. Believe me, I wish that I could, because those mistakes will absolutely have an impact on my legacy. But I also believe that we are spiritual beings making human mistakes. More than ever before, I am working on self-improvement in all areas.

If it seems that I am encouraging failure on the road to success, that is definitely not the case. I am only emphasizing a harsh reality: professional disappointments are woven into the fabric of success far more often than not. Successful people are risk takers, so they inevitably make the wrong choices now and again. But that is exactly what inspires them to do better in the future. Consequently, I strongly believe that people with high levels of ambition should be prepared to make the best of career bungles by distilling the ingrained lessons. Only in that sense do I believe that failure, particularly early in a career, can be beneficial in the grand scheme of things.

Put simply: learning from failure is the key to extracting something positive out of an otherwise negative experience. For example, I learned a lesson early on in my second career as a manager. Perhaps the most important decision when trying to break a new artist is picking the right first single to introduce a debut album. When faced with that daunting task on Destiny's Child eponymous first album, I chose to do something new that would improve my odds. Instead of going with a single, we released two simultaneously. To be precise, we released two versions of the same song—the ballad version of "No, No, No (Part I)" and another specifically for the clubs, "No, No, No (Part 2)," an uptempo remix produced by Wyclef Jean. No matter which version received radio play, the combined count was all that mattered in calculating the song's position on the charts. It shot to number three on the Billboard 100, hit number one on the R&B charts, went platinum—in other words, sold 1 million copies—and won two Soul Train Lady of Soul Awards.

In this chapter, I obviously want to focus on the decisions that did not result in successful outcomes. When I tried the same concept with the second release from *Destiny's Child*, it backfired—bombed, as a matter of fact. "With Me" was selected as the follow-up single to "No, No, No." As for the inevitable club remix that would be released at the same time? We recorded two different versions but released only one. Ultimately, we decided to go with Part 1, not Part 2, despite the fact that the artist featured on Part 2 was then the hottest rap artist of the day. And not only was "With Me" a flop; it proved to be the anchor that sunk the entire project. There was no third single. CD sales stalled.

Remarkably, *Destiny's Child* has barely sold one million copies even to this day. That one wrong decision might have destroyed their career. Sony could have easily cut ties and parted ways with the group—just another girl act who had blown their big opportunity and fell into obscurity. Thankfully, instead of dropping Destiny's Child, Sony agreed to suck up their losses on the debut album and encouraged the girls to go back into the studio. And the rest, as they say, is history: the group's second album, *The Writing's on the Wall*, took them to the next level—international renown—despite all the drama that surrounded their evolving lineup at the time. (More on that in my next book.)

For me, the silver lining was the lesson I learned from that costly mistake: trust my gut. That has been a kind of mantra for me ever since. I learned from my mistake. Looking back, that's all that matters.

I first became acquainted with Troy Carter in the late-1990s, nearly a decade before he became the architect of Lady Gaga's global stardom—her fame, fortune, and social-media mastery—as the eccentric singer's manager. At the time, Troy did not even know Stefani Joanne Angelina Germanotta (Lady Gaga's given name), who was then just a teenager with dreams of becoming a pop sensation. Not that Destiny's Child had found fame yet either—I was still seeking the right opportunity that could result in their big break. I would occasionally see Troy networking at industry events. He was small in stature but big in ideas. He was striking that way.

By 2004, Destiny's Child had caught fire. And so had Troy, especially with one of his first clients: Eve, the rapper-turned-actress. That same year, I sold my company, Music World Entertainment, to Sanctuary, the large independent British music and entertainment company. Subsequently, I was appointed president of a new division, Music World/ Sanctuary Urban. And my first decision was to go out and hire the sharpest young talent managers around. Troy was one person I pursued immediately. We eventually snared him by acquiring Erving Wonder (EW), the Philadelphia-based management company that Troy coowned with J. Erving, son of basketball legend Julius Erving. In addition to Eve, EW handled artists like Angie Stone, Jadakiss, and Floetry.

Troy was always professional. He wanted to learn and was open to being mentored. More than that, he did an exceptional job with follow-through. Troy clearly favored action over talk, which further endeared him to me.

Later, he went on to found Atom Factory, an entertainment management company that focuses as much on technology and branding as music—all three departments work together in perfect harmony. Although he and Lady Gaga have parted ways (to the detriment of her career, I might add), Troy continues to represent John Legend, John

Mayer, Miguel, and Lindsey Stirling, the dubstep violinist and YouTube phenomenon.

Anybody who has enjoyed a long career knows that setbacks are a natural part of life. The real story is in how you get back up and dust yourself off afterward. God has blessed us with pain points: when we make the mistake of touching fire, we learn that it is hot. So I just kind of learned from mistakes as I went along. One of my biggest setbacks? A client I had managed for years came into my office and said, "I'm going in my own direction." This was a client who at the time was basically my entire business. And we did not have a contract. Hurt was my first reaction. You have to understand: talent management is such a personal business that clients become like your family. I went through the different phases—anger, disappointment, regret. I think you have to work through it so that you don't carry any sort of resentment. Once you think it through carefully, you can move forward with your life. It was really important for me to not hold on to any ill will but to move on.

This sudden and unexpected loss gave me the perfect opportunity to rebuild my company and start over from scratch. I learned the hard way that I had to button down my business, for one thing. Handshakes, although they are cool with some people, are not sufficient with everybody. I also learned that I had to start diversifying my organization instead of building it around one client. You know what they say: don't put your eggs all in one basket. One arm of Atom Factory invests in early-stage technology start-ups like Uber, Dropbox, Spotify, and Lyft, to name but a few. The fact of the matter is that we have invested in over fifty companies over the past three years.

But back to that big disappointment: the situation brought me a certain amount of humility as well. I don't take relationships for granted anymore. I learned a lot about the people around me—who was really riding with me versus who was only along for the ride. It goes without saying that there is not a lot of loyalty in this business. All of a sudden my phone stopped ringing. Certain people I used to be able to get on the phone in two seconds would not take my calls. So I paid attention to the people who reached out to me during that time. Many of those are relationships I have had for twenty years, and they are not based on my status in the industry (or my bank account, for that matter). I got a chance to see who the real players were in my life.

I have come to believe that failure is all a matter of perspective. Obviously, I hate to see people lose their job, especially if they have family, children, and people who depend on them. Not everyone can just bounce right back. In that sense, letdowns are not good for everybody. But for people like myself who are a bit more resilient and entrepreneurial, I think it's just part of the gig. Through those setbacks, I was able to put more tools in my toolbox. I learned what I did wrong, but more important, what I did right. I was able to take responsibility and take that information on to the next phase of my career.

Look at a person like Steve Jobs, who was thrown out of Apple. That forced him to look at his career with a different set of eyes. When Steve left, he started Pixar and Next—two great companies—and then came back to Apple with a new perspective and a lot more tools in his toolbox. Or look at Oprah Winfrey. I can go down a list of many other people who have gone through professional setbacks and have used those failures as a catalyst to move forward and go on to do great things.

It is important to find a mentor who has also gone through his or her share of setbacks. Anyone you would consider a professional mentor has surely gone through various career fumbles and inevitable ups and downs. He or she can coach you through the tough times. Just knowing you are not alone is greatly helpful. Yours is not a unique situation. Other people have gone through it as well.

In summation: Setbacks were instrumental to any of my later successes. Honestly, I go through little letdowns once a month. I might go through major ones a few times a year. And we all may feel catastrophic letdowns a few times in our professional lives if we happen to have long careers. I have gone through all of those, and I came out the other side a stronger and wiser man. It has helped me become a better person in general—a better father, a better husband, and a better leader within my organization

Entertainment Tonight was airing when Larry Lorey happened to flip on the TV in his hotel room in Gainesville, where he was visiting his son at the University of Florida. Although he had not seen me in a decade or so, he could have sworn that the face on the screen was mine. When the camera panned to my former wife, Tina, standing next to me onscreen, Larry was certain it was me. But he had no clue why we were on television until Beyoncé appeared between us in the TV image.

Larry was the regional manager I had reported to when I was selling Xerox medical equipment in the late 1970s. (Aside from their success in the field of copy machines, Xerox manufactured a leading scanner for breast cancer.) After a decade of representing the company, I was at the top of my game and earning six figures—a fantastic income in those days, especially for a black man. Then out of the blue one day, I phoned Larry and said, "I'm going to retire and manage my daughter's singing career. She has a lot of talent." I could just imagine what Larry must have thought to himself at the time—yet another delusional dad trying to push his kid into the spotlight, perhaps.

"But you have only worked for Xerox," Larry pointed out as politely as possible. "Who do you know in the music industry for leverage? You have no experience in that marketplace," he added matter-of-factly.

After much consideration, I decided to heed Larry's warning; I had a family to feed, after all. I did end up leaving Xerox, but not to transition into the music business right away. I left in 1988 because the company closed its medical division. I continued to pursue work selling diagnostic imaging equipment—mainly MRI and CT scanners—and trudged along my established career path in corporate America for six more years until 1994.

At the same time, I was working part time as the manager of Girls Tyme. But there came a point when I believed so strongly in their talent that I encouraged the girls to give their music 100 percent. Naturally, I expected nothing less of myself—a manager needs to work at least as hard as his act.

Granted, at that moment in time, I knew practically no one in the music business and little to nothing about the industry itself. Which, in my mind, meant that I would have my share of failures to learn from along the way. Everything would come down to trial and error as I embarked upon my foray into the unknown.

Now flash forward a decade or so. A stagehand delivered a note to me backstage at a Destiny's Child concert in South Florida. Almost immediately, I was on the phone with the sender—Larry Lorey—and later I invited him backstage. "My daddy always says he was the number-one sales rep at Xerox. Is that true?" Beyoncé asked him right off the bat.

Larry, who had been my earliest naysayer, expressed pride in what I had accomplished thanks to Beyoncé's extraordinary talent and unparalleled work ethic. The countless failures in the intervening years yielded valuable lessons about survival and, for me, career revival as Beyoncé rose to the top of the entertainment world.

Since the old days at Xerox, Larry told me, he had suffered numerous highs and lows himself—including at least one nearly catastrophic failure—before he slowly but surely climbed his way back to the top. He is not shy about discussing his accession or the fall that nearly sidelined his career for good.

Once the FBI came knocking at my door after I left Xerox for another work opportunity. As you can imagine, that was not a good sign. It turns out that the guy I went to work for was running a bootleg DVD business on the side, providing labels for illegally copied movies. The sales business was simply a cover. I got out of trouble with the law because I was able to prove that I was not involved and that I had not known anything about the bootleg business, for that matter. Then I cried my way back to Xerox. That is when I moved to California to work for their medical-system division. Then another company ended up wooing me away from Xerox. But I ended up coming back yet again.

I also worked for a medical-equipment company called ResMed in Florida for several years until 2009. We had a specialized treatment for sleep apnea that became number one in the industry. ResMed ended up going public, and the stock split three times. Consequently, I made a ton of money in just a few years' time. Manhattan money managers started calling. "Let me invest your money," they enthusiastically offered. But I did not trust anybody in New York.

Anyway, after four or five years, I had an opportunity to cash in my stock options for a considerable amount. At that time, another persistent money manager got in touch with me. Somewhat reluctantly, I decided to entrust him with $20,000. Much to my surprise, the $20,000 doubled in two weeks! So I promptly turned over the rest of my savings for him to invest.

Thirty days later, it was all gone, every last penny. Keep in mind that I had worked hard my entire life hoping to get to a certain level so that I would never again have to worry about money—or the lack thereof. Finally, I had achieved the American dream: I was going to be a self-made millionaire. Then, just like that, it vanished in less than a month, the whole thing. And I was not the only victim, not by far. My so-called money manager had ripped off a total of $30 million from all of his clients.

Talk about failure. That was the biggest letdown of my entire life! I had let down my entire family, not to mention myself. Suddenly, my hopes and dreams were dashed—all because I made one idiotic mistake by trusting a common thief disguised in a sharp designer suit. Imagine losing everything in thirty days. That was a letdown that literally changed my life. I felt like giving up.

But wallowing in self-pity was not going to feed my family. First of all, I had to look myself in the mirror—which was not easy—and say, "I did it." Whenever you have a setback in life, you cannot deny the fact that it happened. (Unless you choose to be completely delusional and live in denial instead of reality.) You have to man up and say, "I am responsible." Take full accountability. Own it! After all, no one else is to blame for your mistakes. Of course, some people would rather live in denial than admit that they messed up. For those types of delusional people, it's always someone else's fault. But the truth is that you will never go anywhere in life if you are always blaming others for your failures. The real winners in life never let the setback determine whether or not they will ultimately win. Learn from your mistakes, then move on.

I made a lot of mistakes in general by being impatient. Or as my wife politely puts it, "Patience is not your biggest strength." Admittedly, I am an impulsive person by nature, so I have had to learn to think before I act, especially where matters of money are concerned. I now contemplate the potential ramifications of the actions I am considering. In business, you have to think out every step.

Another one of my related problems: I have a big ego. I had to learn to control my ego and keep it in check. If you look at people with the greatest success, they are oftentimes the most humble. Humility is a major asset in business because if you are humble, you remain teachable. The solution required me to take "I" out of the equation and focus on what "we" can accomplish together—"we can" rather than "I can." When you really think about it, no one person really accomplishes all that much alone. No man is an island, as the Bible says.

Failures—and the way that you choose to hastily react or to thoughtfully respond to them—define who you are as a person. My letdowns certainly defined who Larry Lorey is today. I became more humble, more willing to listen to better counsel instead of thinking that I have all the answers. Today, I am not afraid to say when I don't know the answer or to ask for help. I am the first to admit that I am not the smartest person in the world, but I surround myself with the smartest people I know.

Everybody handles failure differently. Letdowns are stressful. They can be devastating or life-changing moments in one's professional career. People are not usually prepared for catastrophic changes—it's not unlike an unexpected earthquake or tsunami. But you have to focus on rebuilding rather than on the damage that has been left behind. And when a letdown comes, you also have to be honest with yourself. Ask yourself: "Did I make a mistake?" or "What part did I play in this mess"?

We are all human, so naturally we have a tendency to shift the blame as a defense mechanism. We tend to look for scapegoats and make excuses for our behavior. But again, every time you encounter a setback—big or little—take time out to evaluate what you did or did not do right. Ask yourself the tough questions: "Why did it happen? What did I do wrong? What can I do to change my situation now?"

I happen to think it is not just valuable but critical to talk about your failures. I have spoken to a lot of friends who have survived serious setbacks in life. When you talk with other people who have experienced similar failures—and if you remain openminded and willing—you can learn from their experiences too. I have a network of people I regularly turn to for a variety of advice—my inner circle, as I like to call it. I can phone them up individually and say, "Hey, let's brainstorm." When you've established a trustworthy network of people you can bounce ideas off of, you can accomplish a lot. Remember: nobody has all the answers. Together we are likely to succeed; alone we are almost certain to fail.

In the fall of 2011, a young woman who looked to be about Beyoncé's age sat next to me on the last flight of the day from New York to Houston. Before long, I asked, "What do you do?" Little did I expect an epic globetrotting story about a music-industry insider that was set partly in Moscow before it took a sharp turn (for the worse) into the boardrooms of two global music giants, Sony and BMG. Her name was Ariana Grinblat, and with my label distributor—Sony—involved, naturally I wanted to know about all the players. I nodded along as she talked.

Ariana revealed herself to be a Russian-American, not to mention a fellow Houstonian. At age fifteen, she became an overnight sensation of sorts after Sony-Russia signed and then relocated her to Moscow in 2000. Even more surprising for a new singer, she managed to maintain creative control, perhaps because her first album generated some of the highest-ever sales for a debut artist. She then became one of the youngest singers to win Russia's equivalent of the Grammy. But Ariana's ambition did not stop there. Her next career move was to transition into a crossover star in the United States. This was the prelude to a failure that robbed her of a once-in-a-lifetime chance—a missed opportunity that made her a wiser woman in the process.

I would consider phase 1 of my career a great success, especially considering the size of a country like Russia in comparison to America. The natural progression was to try to cross me over here in the United States. We had a good team and a successful formula that should have been possible to duplicate—because, after all, I was born in America. Following my relocation to Russia for a few years, I moved to Los Angeles from Moscow in September of 2003. Then things got tricky.

Sony and BMG merged. My Sony A&R person got laid off, and he was replaced by a BMG rep. All the newbie artists, myself included, started falling through the cracks during this corporate shake-up. The team that had been focusing on my project no longer had time for me. Whenever I tried to reach them, I was told that they were busy trying to release a J.Lo album, and that they would get back to me. They never did. So my first big letdown was not being able to cross over in my own country.

The logical—and only—decision was to go back to Russia to work on a new album. I had spent six months in LA while my career peaked in Russia, so I was not there to tour extensively and nurture my success. At the age of eighteen, I simply did not understand. I saw my job as working on my music. I was never involved in the business side of things. When I finally returned to Moscow to record my second album, I wrongly assumed that my audience would be waiting to greet me with open arms. But I found out that fans are fickle and quick to forget.

One of the top executives at Sony-Russia decided that he wanted to be more involved—more hands-on, shall we say—with my next record. He wanted to be a producer. That's fine, I said, because I did not want to be a problem. But before long, we started to clash in terms of the creative vision ... and other areas too. I had never been questioned about the music I was submitting before. But suddenly my demos were getting shot down.

This executive claimed that he did not understand the direction I was going in. Things started to get very tense in our relationship. So I think he just figured, let me find a brand new artist and own 100 percent of the publishing rights. Meanwhile, I felt like I was being sabotaged by someone who was supposed to be on my team.

Suddenly, I was not being invited to attend certain concerts or to participate in television interviews. When it came time to release my second album, the promotional budget was tiny compared to that of my first album, which funded select tour dates around the country, television appearances, and other promotional opportunities. Not surprisingly, radio was not playing my new songs. Whereas I used to hear a lot of yeses, I started hearing a lot of nos. That was pretty much when I decided to take a step back. My album had lost all momentum, and I needed a break. I did not want to lose my love for music.

It was a confusing and frustrating time. I did not understand what was happening. My father was my manager, and I did not have enough life experience to make sense of this situation. It was a rude awakening for me.

Looking back, I have tried to analyze what went wrong. I came into this business as an innocent—wide-eyed and openhearted. Most Texans are raised to be trusting. I must say that I've learned to be careful about the people I trust these days. That was one of the big lessons for me. In this business, the only people you should try to be honest with is your audience, and the way you do that is through your music. With everyone else, wear a poker face and be careful about showing your cards.

I used to wear my emotions on my sleeve. It was because I was so young—I started out at the age of fourteen. I had no experience in show business or everyday life, for that matter. I had to learn my lessons in the public eye. Honestly, I did my best to get through it all with grace and dignity. And I am grateful for everything that I have learned. I will carry my lessons into the future, and they will prove to be invaluable.

In a sense, I feel lucky to have learned such hard lessons about the music business when I was relatively young. I still have plenty of time to make an amazing comeback. Also, I have to keep reminding myself that I did a lot of incredible things. Rarely does everything go according to plan. So the earlier you see the drawbacks, the sooner you can adjust accordingly. You need to recognize the limitations and figure out a way to transcend them. You have to be honest about the part you played in the failure too.

I know plenty of people who have endured professional disappointments. You hear about people in the tech world who experienced multiple failures before they honed in on one great idea that eventually took off. Some people may not think it is productive to discuss things that have gone wrong. You can sit in denial and blame the entire world while wallowing in your failure. That can become all-consuming. But the fact is that if you are mature enough to discuss what went wrong, that means you are more likely to make the next endeavor a success. I have found it very helpful to talk about—and to learn from—my career missteps.

I believe that I have a definite advantage now. For instance, I have more awareness of how to build my career on my own. I can move forward and make educated and informed decisions at this point. I know what to expect, and that is very helpful. Sometimes people can get so enamored with the idea of success that they refuse to see the flaws in a plan. The first thing you need to do when analyzing a business venture is ask: What are all the worst-case scenarios? What are the possible flaws? I have always been honest with myself. It's who I am.

While recording, I was still in high school. But I was accepted by Brown University as well as UC Berkeley and Boston University. I chose to defer a year from Brown—my top choice—when I moved to Los Angeles to start recording my potential crossover album. I never did end up going, because the following year I moved back to Moscow to record another album for the Russian market. I ended up getting my bachelor's from the University of Massachusetts through their distance learning program, which allowed me to continue my career at full speed and still move toward my goal of a college degree.

I am currently living in New York City, and in February of 2014, I opened my own restaurant, Ariana, in SoHo. I developed the entire concept as well as the menu myself. Opening a restaurant has been a dream of mine for a while. I am an avid foodie, but as much as I like to experiment as a diner, I have just as much fun in the kitchen. This restaurant is an expression of my culture and a reflection of my perspective as a modern Russian American. So many Russian restaurants play on outdated stereotypes—gimmicks of what people perceive Russia to be like.

Especially after the Sochi Winter Olympics, it is time to redefine the

Russia that actually is—notorious nightlife, top-notch dining, art, fashion, the list goes on and on. This is my Russia, and I like to think of the restaurant as an extension of my living room.

For the past six months, my focus has been on the restaurant, but I do still write and record when time allows. I am also one of the founders of a Russian record label based in Moscow called the BitRate Group. These days, I work more on the producing and talent-development end. In fact, one of our artists recently opened for Lana Del Rey during her Moscow performance. So I am certainly not done with my music career. After all, I am only twenty-eight years old. This isn't the end of the road for me, not by a long shot.

Quiz: Learning from Failure

This is a trait that most people struggle with, so I ask for your complete honesty on this one.

1. What is your definition of failure?

2. Recall three of your biggest failures in life. Write them down in detail.

3. Why do you think that you failed in each one of those three instances?

4. Looking over your answers to the second question, do you recognize any similar characteristics—or, rather, character defects—in all three cases? If so, write them down.

5. What cumulative lessons have you learned from your past experiences with failure?

6. How can these lessons help you move forward—and become even more successful—in the future?

9

Giving Back

In my mind, a successful person and a charitable person are one in the same. Granted, there is no scientific proof of this phenomenon, though I highly doubt that any researchers have even investigated a potential link. But there certainly is "Mathew's Proof": in over thirty years of crossing paths with highly successful people—including, of course, my superstar daughters—I have rarely come face to face with a high-achieving person who did not give back in one form or another. In fact, all the successful folks I will introduce in the forthcoming pages will attest to my theory. As a result, I am confident that success is impossible to achieve, or rather maintain, with an uncharitable and greedy heart. Giving back just comes naturally to folks who are blessed with an avalanche of accomplishment.

In the spirit of giving back, most successful people offer to others the helping hand that they received while climbing the long ladder of success. For example, at Xerox, where I first made my mark as a salesman, there is no way that I could have mastered the art of selling without a great mentor—and mine was a man by the name of Worth Davis. The fact that Worth gave of himself for the benefit of boosting my personal quest to be the best was an invaluable act of charity for which I will be forever grateful. During his fourteen years with Xerox, Worth earned thirteen national sales and management awards as well as recognition as the Southern Region Branch Manager of the Year. He had much to offer an eager upstart like myself. I remember those days when I would get to work around seven o'clock in the morning just to get Worth's *Wall Street Journal* to read, which was just outside the office door. Worth started stopping by my sales cubby hole to see who had gotten his *Wall Street*, which led to our morning conversations about current business trends. Those were invaluable mentorship moments for me.

Naturally, I am now following in his footsteps. And I believe that my mentoring will help to propel the people I have the pleasure of teaching to reach loftier professional heights. Many of them are thriving already, as a matter of fact. For example: in 2004, Music World/Sanctuary Urban, where I was then president, bought Erving Wonder, the management firm that represented hip-hop stars including rap recording artist Eve. One of the owners, Troy Carter—who you met in chapter 8—stayed on, and he reported directly to me. For a time, Troy managed none other than Lady Gaga, one of the most exciting, successful, and beloved pop stars in the world. I would hope that some of his own success came from the fact that I served as his mentor.

A generous heart as a youngster does not guarantee that a kid will grow up to be a great success story. And yet charity began early in life for most successful people in my circle of friends. Somewhere along the way, they inevitably had a role model for giving back. I vividly recall my parents, who were unimaginably hardworking, helping out our neighbors in Gadsden, Alabama, whenever possible. My father worked two or three jobs to keep our family afloat, but he also had a CB radio, and late at night he could often be found listening for car accidents or house fires in case he had to run for help. Because he was so big, he could carry the hoses, whereas it would usually take at least two other men. My mom would constantly be making quilts at home and then giving them out to the needy at Thanksgiving and Christmas. Reverend Walker, my childhood family minister and godfather, also gave back to others—his time, his money, and his loving advice. I grew up in that kind of selfless environment. Many successful people can tell similar stories.

Apart from a natural feel-good sensation, giving back doesn't produce instant gratification for givers, if any return at all. But then, we don't expect some big payday from our well-meaning donations. Successful folks realize that their charity would be a cynical gesture if they were motivated by the expectation of anything in return. In many cases, they have achieved success because others gave to them—an opportunity, a referral, even a recommendation or insightful suggestion. Truly successful people give back because they feel (by which I mean that they know in their hearts) it is the right thing to do. It's no more complex or complicated than that. They want to do good by others, plain and simple. Because they can.

It should not surprise you, either, that successful people have no desire for any return on their charitable endeavors other than the recipient's best use of what is freely given. I, for one, have never wanted or needed to be rewarded for giving back. I don't personally know Warren Buffett, who is friendly with my daughter, Beyoncé, and my son-in-law, Jay Z. Yet I ask you, what could the third richest person in the world want in return for giving away his fortune, as he has famously pledged to do? Perhaps to be remembered as a great American philanthropist.

Still, all of my successful friends and acquaintances will confess to this: they have harvested a bounty of positive karma and goodwill that generosity always seems to inspire. I believe that in our universe, kindness toward others sets off a chain reaction that causes good things to flow back in the direction of the benevolent. Big-hearted successful people tell me this all the time. And by good things, I don't necessarily mean more fame, fortune, or accomplishment. Spiritually, I think you get something in return every single time you give back. You might never put two and two together—that you've actually gained something from giving back. Or it might take a while before you understand and relate to my line of thinking.

A case in point is the payoff I got from an impromptu donation I once made to a nun who was collecting funds in a cup at Los Angeles International Airport. I gave her whatever I had in my pocket, a few hundred dollars. She looked at me with a tear in her eye, and she gave me a card that I put in my pocket without reading it. Maybe a week or so later, I was at a car wash in Houston when I looked at the back of this card for the first time. It said: "Pray not for a life free from trouble. Pray for triumph over trouble. For what you and I call adversity, God calls opportunity."

That really touched me. We are always praying that no bad stuff ever happens to us. But this card was advising me to not do that for the sake of spiritual growth, which only comes through an uncomfortable struggle of some sort. In other words, don't say prayers to block unfortunate events. Instead, pray to triumph over seemingly bad events that inevitably happen in everyone's life. I once heard a wise man say that we often reject gifts from God simply because we don't like the wrapping paper; make of that what you will.

I started looking at life—and, specifically, its meaning—from a much different perspective after that. I began looking at how I could overcome and grow stronger as a result of my own troubles, how I could turn a negative into a positive simply by shifting my outlook. My attitude was irreparably altered by the message on that piece of paper.

The overwhelming majority of my own giving back is on display in Houston. Of course, because of the global stardom of Destiny's Child and

Beyoncé's skyrocketing solo career, we have shared the fruits of our labors far beyond our own hometown. Still, Houston was the springboard for the success that we've been fortunate enough to earn and to experience, so it stands to reason that our giving back has been concentrated there primarily. Not to mention that we felt obliged to meet the hometown expectation to share our good fortune with locals who supported us—and believed in us—from the very beginning.

Like countless successful people who give back, we are most proud of the contributions we can make toward the betterment of our neighbors, and that's where we best understand the greatest need and can have the strongest impact. That's the thought process behind the charitable inclinations of most successful folks I happen to know. So our best giving back has been in Houston, largely in partnership with our place of worship, St. John's United Methodist Church, as well as through our entertainment company and nonprofit foundation.

Generally, we have concentrated on at-risk youth, the homeless, and victims of disasters, natural or otherwise. But it's impolite, I believe, to rattle on about what—and how much money—we happen to give. My minister, Rev. Rudy Rasmus, whom you will meet a bit later on in this chapter, can more appropriately discuss this matter.

There is one particularly fun example that I cannot resist detailing though. In the past during every holiday season, Music World and the label's Survivor Foundation would cosponsor the Music World Cares Holiday Carnival, an event for kids. We would erect an amusement park on the property and Santa makes a surprise appearance to gives out toys to less fortunate children. Our other special guest, Tyson Foods, the major meat company, participates by contributing an eighteen-wheeler truck filled with free hams for the hungry.

Moreover, teaching for me is a vital form of giving back that brings me great joy and particular pride, not to mention an indescribable feeling of fulfillment. I currently teach courses on the music business in the School of Communications called the Recording Industry and Artist Management, as well as Introduction to Entrepreneurship in the

School of Business at Texas Southern University, one of the nation's largest historically black colleges and universities. Whenever my schedule allows, I also give motivational speeches at, among other places, USC's Department of Music, Berklee College of Music in Boston, and Nashville's Fisk University, my alma mater. But I don't teach for money. I teach for a spiritually rewarding paycheck because I see these kids engaged and inspired as a result of my instruction. I see their willingness to learn new things, which inspires me as well. I see their passion developing right before my eyes, and I get to be a small part of their educational journey and personal development. It brings me utter joy. It gave me the inspiration at age sixty-three to get my MBA and soon my PhD.

At the end of the last "The Recording Industry" course, one of my students came to the front of the class and said he wanted to make a brief announcement. There was something different about this student; he was walking tall with his shoulders back and with an air of self-confidence. This was the same student who had been late for class a couple times during the semester and each time—almost in tears—had explained that he was tardy because was needed at home to take care of his brother and sister. "What do you mean?" I'd asked him.

"My mom and dad don't take care of us. I take care of my brother and sister both," he responded with his head down, unable to make eye contact with me. "I had to take them from my parents." I respectfully left it at that and didn't ask any more intrusive questions.

"Nobody knows this, and I think Mr. Knowles may have forgotten," the formerly shy student announced, proudly standing at the head the class. "But Mr. Knowles bought me and my parents a home when he worked with Habitat for Humanity five years ago. That home is where I continue to live. My parents got kicked out, but I was able to stay there and take care of my little brother and sister. You didn't know this, Mr. Knowles, but I just wanted to thank you for the fact that we have a place to live."

It had never dawned on me that the student and I had actually met before, and definitely not under the circumstances he had just described.

I now remember meeting the family only once four or five years earlier. And he would have been a little guy then—barely a teenager. To say that this resulted in a touching moment for the class and especially for me is an understatement.

I've had the good fortune of meeting many, many people whose success derived from giving back. One such person is Nancy Brown, chief executive of the American Heart Association and a twenty-six-year veteran of the organization. For several years now, I have heard her talk about the importance of giving to the community as I have become increasingly familiar with her lifelong dedication to nonprofit organizations.

Nancy's mission in life is helping others. I joined her cause when I was asked to be an ambassador of the organization's Power to End Strokes. This was a cause initiative that Nancy launched in 2006 to raise awareness about strokes, a major health risk for everybody. But with Power to End Strokes, Nancy focused specifically on African Americans. As it turns out, we are twice as likely as white people to suffer strokes in our lifetimes. Four of every ten African Americans—I'm one of them, incidentally—have high blood pressure.

At Music World, we partnered with the heart-health charity in 2010. That's when I became an ambassador, which is to say that I am a very active and outgoing volunteer. Among other things, we participated in a concert at the legendary Apollo Theater in Harlem that gave top billing to the Power to End Strokes message, and my label's artists served as ambassadors too, for Nancy's impassioned initiative. Charity has always defined who she is, she says.

Giving back is a way of life for me. From the time I was a little girl in Michigan (I grew up about an hour north of Detroit), my mother was an active community volunteer. She instilled in me and my sisters the importance of serving others as opposed to being self-serving and self-seeking. I spent a lot of time as a youngster volunteering and raising money for a variety of different causes.

I distinctly remember being five or six years old when my mother was the block captain in charge of raising money for the March of Dimes. I would go door to door along with Mom, talking to our friends and neighbors and telling the story of the charity's roots as an organization and how it impacted people's lives. We explained to our neighbors how and why their commitment to donate and financial gifts would make a difference and improve the lives of others. Connecting with our neighbors on that level—and giving them an opportunity to share their wealth with a truly wonderful organization—made an imprint on me that has obviously lasted until today.

In my mind, giving back absolutely fuels success. I believe that a life that has other people—as opposed to yourself—at the center of it is richer in every sense of the word. You spend more time thinking about how to give back, whether it's the resource of your time, mentoring young people, or helping out with community-strengthening organizations. All of that brings a great sense of calm, serenity, and leadership that helps broaden a giving person's experiences, not to mention expand his or her network. It helps a person feel accomplished in a way that will never be possible for selfish people who are driven to think about only their own desires and personal possessions. In my experience, the most successful people choose to live their lives by this philosophy. They inevitably get back so much more than they give.

My world is filled with people who live to give back, people who have dedicated their professional careers to philanthropic organizations that have at their core a belief in giving to others and making communities stronger, richer, better. I have the fortunate experience of being surrounded by people who share that belief—that passion—which I also have.

While successful people don't necessarily plan their giving, it's not exactly arbitrary either. I believe things come along in life that make an impression on us, whether it's the lingering impact of a disease, illness, or other health issue that someone in our family—or we ourselves—have faced, or an awakening or spiritual gathering, or maybe it's something that surfaces in the community. Things happen that make a profound difference, and people realize they can impact the situation by donating their time and resources, even if all they have to offer at the end of the day is hope. Hope matters. These are a few of the reasons why successful people eventually focus on giving back. They come to understand the broader impact that they can have not only for themselves but also for their community.

For me, the values of philanthropy are first and foremost in my life, and I am grateful that I was able to build a successful career based on my beliefs. I'm the kind of person who has been attracted to this type of work from the very beginning. I have had numerous wonderful opportunities to explore my passion throughout my entire career. I think these things must be like magnets. People who have like-minded principles are attracted to places where they can live their values. That certainly is something that happened to me. As I grew and went through my studies in college and later business school, there was never a doubt that I would find a way to use my skills to help others. What I have gained in return is truly immeasurable.

Charity, as that familiar saying goes, begins at home. Practically all the generous and successful people represented in this book have substantiated that point, but few more so than my pastor, Rudy Rasmus. More precisely, he is copastor with his wife, Juanita, of St. John's United Methodist Church in Houston.

Rudy and I first met about three decades ago. In his own words, Rudy was a "marginal gangster" in his former life. In those days, we'd see each other on the club scene, which was about as far from holy as one could get. Obviously, Rudy was rehabilitated, and his life changed radically. He found God, became a Christian, and eventually accepted his unanticipated calling to ministry. In 1992, he founded St. Johns with nine other members, myself and family included.

Today, it happens to be one of the nation's most culturally diverse fellowships. The membership has grown to more than ten thousand, of which three thousand are—or were at one time—homeless. They are the segment of Rudy's flock to which he has given back at a level that is difficult to overstate. In the process, Rudy has helped guide many of us along the path of philanthropy. In short: giving back is central to his being. And he would be the first to enthusiastically tell you this.

The core nature of what I do in the community is about reaching out to the least capable members. My core ethos is about identifying the greatest need in the room and moving quickly toward that need. Stewardship in the nonprofit and spiritual communities is often about doing something for someone or helping a person who in many cases may never be able to repay you or, in even more cases, have the opportunity to thank you. Those who are philanthropic at heart understand that most of what we do for others will go unnoticed. But we consider ourselves blessed to have the opportunity to be of service, especially when no one else is looking.

In my own charitable endeavors, I interact with a vast array of successful people who are a part of my congregation. I have discovered that more often than not, they have faced deprivation, harsh challenges, and personal struggles not unlike the needy that they now seek to assist and to empower. We have raised probably $100 million for charity over the last decade, beginning at the turn of the century. Those funds came from people who were able to identify and relate to being without for long periods of time before their luck turned. The philanthropic heart is often at the center of a compassionate person who can empathize with the pain and suffering of others. I think the most generous people I've ever encountered in service to their community are people willing to remember where they came from—and how their lives have not always been as good as they are now. Their old lives didn't necessarily reflect the success of their current state. It's essentially about one person looking at others and saying, "They too are attempting to find peace, joy, and happiness. But unlike me, that person might not have the skill set, connections, or opportunities."

Perhaps my early experience with racism put me on the path to make sure that others were not similarly discriminated against. After all, I grew up drinking from a separate water fountain marked "Colored." Out of the pain and resentment of being segregated came my desire to see that no human being would be marginalized because of skin color or socioeconomic circumstances, not if I could help it. This mostly involves helping people find hope and see the possibility of a better life in the future.

My history of giving back in Houston is most visible in a three-block radius anchored by St. John's in the city's downtown. The first project we launched was a center for young people—the Knowles–Rowland Center for Youth. It's a multipurpose recreational complex that is named for Mathew's family and for Kelly Rowland, one of the original members of Destiny's Child. We kept moving, kept growing, kept building, and through the years we took on more and more service to the community. At one point, we decided to combat the epidemic of homelessness by constructing affordable housing as well. And so the Knowles–Temenos Place Apartments opened in 2009. They are efficiency apartments, forty-three in all. This facility features an array of support services, everything from assistance with job-hunting to improving work skills and nutrition. Tenants who get a key have to hit the ground running in order to create a life for themselves. We've literally seen lives turn around. We have therefore seen the power—and possibilities—of community.

Mathew has been a vital member of the community-building process. He brought his particular skill set and capabilities to bear on the mission to help people who were living outdoors and specifically underprivileged young people. From the moment he walked through the door, Mathew has been nothing but magnanimous. He was generous with his time despite his crazy schedule. He was always willing to show support and to give whatever he could.

This was before, way before, he made his millions in wealth from the entertainment business. Over the years, he has contributed more than $5 million to projects in and around the church. Many contributions have been life changing for people in need—desperate need. Having been close to Mat for as long as I have, what I know for a fact is that he comprehends the meaning of generosity, and he understands it because of his origins in Alabama. He nurtured the careers of his daughters, who have been wildly successful. But there has been a great deal of sacrifice that had to take place to see those careers flourish and blossom.

I have to come to believe that a clenched fist cannot receive. Unless your hand is open—by which I mean unless your heart is open—you are not going to get anything in return. By anything, I mean spiritual riches. Years ago, when we were building a big soup kitchen and shower facility for the homeless, another wealthy friend, Jack Blanton, shared a key lesson with me. He said, "Rudy, nobody in this life makes it alone. We all need—and, hopefully, receive—help somewhere along the way. Somebody opens a door, relates an opportunity, or simply makes an introduction. The appropriate response to lavish generosity is, yes, generosity. You have to reconcile the fact that you didn't make it on your own. Because the reality is, you made it because someone was kind enough to give you a break and hook you up. So the best reaction to someone hooking you up is to lend a hand to someone else." The Bible said it best: "Give and it shall be given unto you." Reciprocity is a powerful thing. Very powerful indeed.

One thing's for sure in this world: you will be asked to give at some point, especially if you have the financial resources. What I always suggest is to give out of your passion. And that passion can be out of a relationship or out of an opportunity. For instance, I think the more you have, the more responsibility you also have with your bounty. There's that adage: "To whom much is given, much is required." The more you have, the more responsibility you have in managing your philanthropy appropriately. Personally, I recommend giving intentionally and thoughtfully. You can bet that if I had more money, I'd be even more intentional and thoughtful. The more access to assets one has, the more deliberate that person should be about the redistribution of their wealth, in my opinion.

Take Warren Buffett. He has already given away a ton and evidently will not be satisfied until he gives away the entirety of his enormous fortune. But he did not walk down the street and randomly give handouts to strangers. He gave to Microsoft founder Bill Gates, whom he knew was doing the same and had done it successfully.

Giving is, after all, an investment—and the best possible return on that investment is the improvement of another person's life. So when you give, hell yes you want to see tangible proof of lives impacted. As a result, you want to see the culture affected. Improved. And evolved.

Hunger is perhaps our nation's most outrageous social failure. Tens of millions of citizens—including vast numbers of malnourished children—struggle every day to find their next meal. Fortunately, in recent years, that struggle has been a little less desperate thanks to Vicki Escarra. From 2006 until the summer of 2012, Vicki was president and chief executive officer of Feeding America, the nation's number one hunger-relief charity. In July of 2012, she continued her career investment in the top ranks of nonprofits when she was appointed CEO of Opportunity International, a micro-financing organization that provides access to savings, small-business loans, insurance, and training in the developing world.

I first met Vicki during discussions that resulted in Beyoncé's promotion of "Show Your Helping Hand," a hunger relief initiative launched by Feeding America in 2009. Among other things, Vicki and I talked about the importance for Beyoncé of giving back.

A native of Georgia who grew up in a family that didn't have much aside from love, Vicki was repeatedly exposed to the problem of hunger throughout her childhood—it literally hit home. But even then, giving back was second nature to her. She rose above her humble background to become a senior executive at Delta Airlines for thirty years and served briefly as a top aide to former Atlanta mayor Shirley Franklin. As Vicki's circumstances changed, so too did her level of commitment to philanthropy, as she eloquently relates.

I tried to live up to this whole notion of giving back every day. I'm keenly aware of—and very grateful for—all I have been blessed with in my life. I grew up in a family that was for the most part lower-income. I can't forget that hunger was a reality we struggled with every day of my childhood. My grandparents were both farmers, you see. There wasn't a lot of money, but plenty of love to go around. We learned the importance of giving back to neighbors who didn't have as much as we had. Farmers knew how to take care of their own.

At our church, we were always taking collections to provide meals for people who were sick or recently had babies. It was just that kind of caring environment. I think there's a natural sense of wanting to help others if you grow up not having a lot. It's pretty easy to understand people who are just one paycheck away from losing any type of security—or absolutely everything.

I understand and appreciate how fortunate I am to have had the opportunities that came my way—a very successful career at Delta Airlines, for instance, and this wonderful, meaningful work I have been able to do at Feeding America. That feeling of community, that life is not just about working to support your own family but about making room for those who are less fortunate, is a core value of mine. I fully recognize that we as a global community are more connected than ever before and not isolated, not alone in this world.

Based on the time I've had at Feeding America, which was nearly seven years in all, it's more difficult and challenging work than any position I ever held in the private sector. But I actually got more out of it. There's something indescribable about helping people who can do nothing to repay an act of kindness. Does it make you successful? It depends on how you define success. It certainly connects you to the community—and the world—we live in. I can attest that it really grounds me as a human being.

There's a great quote I love by Paul Newman, about the benevolence and the brutality of luck. It's just luck that any of us was born in the United States, for instance. We could have been born in the Congo or in a million other places where people don't have the opportunity to be successful. So if you keep that in mind—the idea that luck is the first step—then hard work, good leadership, and education play a big role in being successful. But it all begins with luck, right? That keeps me grounded.

My experience suggests that while the overwhelming majority of successful people are naturally prone to giving back, some of them need to be motivated or at least inspired. It depends on their upbringing. People who were brought up to give back typically fall in line. And Americans are very generous compared to other nationalities and cultures, anyway. This country was built on an authentic sense of volunteerism, after all. But you can get people involved in abstract causes like hunger if they can just make—and feel—a connection. Once they get involved and have a chance to familiarize themselves with the people they are serving, there's no going back. They are usually involved and committed for life from that point onward.

I think often when a crisis hits, like Katrina or this ongoing financial crisis, it really helps organizations like Feeding America connect with communities and get people to respond. The destruction caused by Katrina actually resulted in a miraculous time of growth for us. We had been raising about $28 million annually until then. But after Katrina and the outreach efforts, followed by the pain and suffering and devastation that people witnessed on the nightly news, we experienced a massive surge in donations that totaled nearly $37 million. It really opened the door for Feeding America and, I would say, shone a light on who we were and what we do and what our mission is.

An interesting question is: are people born or built to give back? Research indicates that the majority of successful people are planning to give back. But when you look at the broader base of people—people who are middle-income givers—they simply don't plan as much. Therefore, they connect emotionally with situations like a crisis or natural disaster. It's worth noting that in terms of other national charity organizations, everybody else's giving has gone down since the onset of the financial crisis. The giving at Feeding America, however, has been up close to 75 percent. The largest giving we've seen happens to be from middle-income people who care deeply about their neighbors. If you can connect a charity to your neighbor, friend, church, community, or some issue that may have changed your life—breast cancer, diabetes, hunger—people will be motivated to give. At the end of the day, I believe that's just our nature.

Quiz: Giving Back

I am a believer in the old saying, "When much is given, much is received." We have the opportunity to give our time, our money, our friendship, and our love in many different ways. This chapter is about helping others who might not be as fortunate as we are.

1. List the variety of ways that you have assisted others in the past.

2. List the reasons you were motivated to offer your help in those instances.

3. List a few of the greatest things you wish to be remembered for.

4. For each item in the question above, explain why.

5. After carefully reviewing your responses, ask yourself this question: Do you feel that you have done enough to help others in the past?

6. If you hesitated on the question above—or if your answer was no— then what more could you do to help others in the immediate future?

— 10 —

Thinking Outside the Box

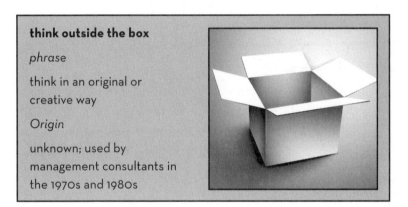

think outside the box

phrase

think in an original or
creative way

Origin

unknown; used by
management consultants in
the 1970s and 1980s

S ometimes it takes an outsider to see things from a different perspective. When I first started out in the music business, I felt imprisoned by boxed-in thinking. Everywhere I turned, I was slamming into archaic industry conventions and banging my head against the walls. Take singles, for example, which are the bread and butter of the industry. No, I was constantly told, there could only be one single at a time—not two—just one song released within a specific window of time. This was according to industry standard, practice, custom, whatever. But as an outsider—a former peddler of market-leading office and diagnostic medical equipment—what did I know? I thought differently.

Consider also my entrepreneurial venture in the beauty industry: Headliners Salon, where we made our first million dollars. Our largely female client base—the African American elite—was the envy of other hair salons. We attracted upwardly mobile professional women and high-income earners: doctors, lawyers, and corporate executives, plus the wives (and girlfriends) of famous athletes. These types of customers were accustomed to being pampered, so we offered them an array of glamorous amenities, from fine wine and champagne to phone and fax lines and any other service that a modern-day multitasker might need.

At this time, in the 1980s, I was still working for Xerox Medical Systems and making my foray into selling medical diagnostic equipment, which required me to understand the needs of radiologists. Note that I borrowed the concept for my business model from corporate America, not the creative arena.

Think about when you walk into a doctor's office: The first person you see is the receptionist, who hands you a questionnaire to fill out. The goal is to get a historical view of you as a new client. Similarly, we needed to understand our clients. We wanted information about your annual service expectations. Were you going to be a $200 a year customer or someone who spends upward of $20,000 annually? Such key data was always at our fingertips because Headliners was fully computerized, which was a rarity for the time. Also, we were curious to know what products you used, much the same way that your doctor asks what medication you take and if you have any allergies. Obviously, the doctor does not want to prescribe something that might result in a bad reaction. Nobody wants to be sued for malpractice, and you had better believe that we took the hair business every bit as seriously as doctors practice medicine.

The next thing that happens in a doctor's office is a nurse enters the waiting room to greet you and says, "Please follow me." After escorting you to a private room, she asks, "So why are you here today?" You might say something like, "I woke up with a cold," while the nurse checks your temperature, blood pressure, and weight. She notes all the relevant information for the doctor and puts your chart on a rack outside the door.

This was the procedure in our salon: An assistant greeted you and asked which stylist you were there to see and what service you required. "A relaxer and a cut," a customer might have responded. The assistant then introduced the customer to the stylist, who looked over the chart and recommended a special type of relaxer for the assistant to use. We only hired high-level assistants who could handle coloring and relaxing as well as shampooing; the ratio of assistants to stylists was two to one, which ensured excellent customer service. I never wanted the hairstylists to leave their designated chairs; they were paid for their expertise, which was cutting and styling. After a customer's service was complete, the stylist put her in the chair and went to work, keeping in mind that her client did not want to spend all day long getting her hair done. We took pride in the fact that the length of stay in our salon was the lowest in the city—that was our reputation, anyway.

Product sales accounted for around 40 percent of our revenue, which necessitated frequent inventories and well-stocked shelves. Just like a doctor might prescribe medication to patients, every stylist wrote a recommendation for the client: a deep-penetrating conditioner, for instance, along with instructions to use it every day for at least fifteen minutes. The bulk of the business was, of course, shampoo and conditioner, but we sold everything from mousse (this was the 1980s, after all) to hairspray, kids' products, cosmetics, and an array of nail polishes. We were the first black hair salon to use Paul Mitchell products almost exclusively; we positioned ourselves as an upscale African American business. In fact, Headliners was the first African American business of any kind established in the Montrose area of Houston—the cultural center of the city where the museums are located.

The staff consisted of a head stylist, hairstylists, receptionists, a floor manager, an aesthetician, nail technicians, and many, many assistants. We treated all of our employees with the utmost respect because even the receptionists played a crucial role at Headliners. Whenever anyone called to make an appointment, it was up to the receptionist to determine why she was coming in and what services were required—clearly making sure to collect as much information and data as possible.

Fast-forward to 1998. Finally, *Destiny's Child*, the eponymous debut album, had been completed. "No, No, No," a ballad, was scheduled to be the first single. And who happened to be in Houston at the time but Wyclef Jean of the Fugees, one of the hottest and freshest groups around at the time. I begged Wyclef, and he eventually agreed to do a remix of "No, No, No." But the session got off to a bad start, to put it mildly. Wyclef showed up at the studio ninety minutes late—on a morning when he had to catch a flight back to New York

Beyoncé was understandably unhappy. Like a true professional, she did not verbalize her feelings, but they were evident in her tone as she raced through the lyrics at what seemed like warp speed. Time was tight, after all. Wyclef instantly perked up at her breakneck tempo. "What did you just do?" Wyclef asked in disbelief. "Do it again!" And that is the story of how Beyoncé effortlessly birthed what would become her trademark style of rap-singing, which was nothing shot of revolutionary for both the R&B and pop genres at the time. I firmly believe that her fast and tough staccato rhymes would still hold up today against any female MC in the business.

From this spontaneous burst of frustration-fueled creativity, how would I get a number-one record? And, ideally, nearly as fast as Beyoncé's vocal delivery? At that moment in the studio, an out-of-the-box thought came to mind: Why don't we put the remix and the original ballad on the album and count them together as one track, no matter which version gains airplay and rules on the radio? This was unprecedented for a first single on a debut album by any artist or group. The usual process, according to so-called conventional wisdom, would be to put the ballad on the album, get airplay for it, and then midway through the radio cycle release the stand-alone remix.

Sony "suits"—as music execs are generically known—laughed off my idea, literally. "Ha, ha! You're funny," they chuckled. "People don't put remixes on albums. Who would do that?" I recall being asked. *An innovator,* I thought to myself. This is when I phoned Broadcast Data System (BDS), the Nielsen information service that monitors radio, television, and Internet play of music. Raw BDS data determines how songs stack up on the Nielsen-owned Billboard charts. In tallying up total plays, would BDS count Part 1 (a ballad) and Part 2 (the remix) as one and the same—alternate tempos, same lyrics? Or would each be a distinctive, and different, single?

So what if no one had ever asked? BDS deliberated and, as it turned out, endorsed what I had believed from the beginning: two versions of the same song. And what a song it was: "No, No, No" hit number one on the Billboard Hot R&B/Hip-Hop chart and number three on the Billboard Hot 100 chart. By thinking outside the box, we not only achieved our goal—we actually surpassed it.

Because of its metaphorical nature, thinking outside the box is not an exact science, nor is it an idea that can be explained with any precision. But several years ago, when I was teaching at the Berklee College of Music, one of the world's most prestigious centers for music education, I devised a way to demonstrate the concept. It all began with a simple command: "Get in the box!"

It was not ominous, despite how it might have sounded to the four meek-looking student volunteers who had initially seemed so eager when I beckoned them to the stage in a packed auditorium. The box, which served as my visual aid, could fit four. My initial volunteer entered first, followed by three friends she had invited to join her onstage at my behest. "Walk around inside the box," I instructed them, but their shuffling feet went nowhere fast. "Impossible, right? The walls are inhibiting your mobility. They are stopping you in your tracks. Walls," I added, "are the conditions that require us to operate within certain confines."

All four students demonstrated the frustrating equivalent of boxed-in thinking. Just as walls limit movement, so too does boxed-in thinking constrain creativity. The box would have been confining for just the first volunteer. And after she was joined by three fellow students, it proved to be a very tight squeeze indeed—a temporary prison, in fact. Ultimately, of course, I allowed my volunteers to get out of their cardboard confines.

Naturally, they could then move and walk around. Without walls, their creativity was free-flowing and limitless.

Of the ten traits I have recognized as common denominators among super-successful people, this skill may be the most challenging to develop and nurture. That is in part because many, if not most, of us have been conditioned to not extend ourselves beyond certain parameters. We are instructed to acknowledge and accept boundaries within the workplace, for instance. We are told to stick with the "tried and true" and to avoid "reinventing the wheel"—because, after all, "if it ain't broke, don't fix it."

I believe that an ongoing effort to foster innovative thinking fuels the fire of creativity. Hit songs do not write themselves, after all; they take time and, most important, effort. There is even an organization that is dedicated to the cause of promoting outside-the-box thinking—the Creative Thinking Association of America. Its mission: "to awaken and stimulate the creative urge in all of us by providing resources for unleashing human potential."

As with so many sayings, it is unclear who first coined the phrase "thinking outside the box." But according to my research, there seems to be a consensus that it came into popular use among management consultants in the 1970s and 1980s, and that it has roots in the so-called "nine-dot puzzle." Consultants would challenge clients to link the nine dots with four (or fewer) single straight lines. As the illustration below indicates, one solution involves extending lines beyond—or, rather, outside—the "box" to form an umbrella-like shape.

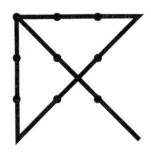

For me, it was fitting that Berklee served as the backdrop for my first demonstration of what I have learned about thinking outside the box—and how the concept can be applied in all aspects of life. In the professional world, I channeled my most prolific and groundbreaking creative thinking once I officially became a part of the music industry. I may have been a fish out of water, so to speak, but I quickly learned how to walk, run, and, yes, fly.

As you may recall, my career began in sales, hawking copiers for Xerox and, later, medical diagnostic equipment for Xerox Medical, Picker International, and Philips, among others. Thanks to my combination of hustle, ability to consistently meet or exceed customers' expectations, and exhaustive knowledge of my product, I was destined to succeed. Sales forces today in every industry are constantly in search of innovative techniques for identifying potential customers and sealing deals. Back in the day, however, not so much creative thinking was necessary to succeed in sales. Having the novel thought to come into the office on Fridays—something most salespeople did not do at the time, if you can believe it—was about the greatest stretch of outside-the-box thinking required in my meteoric rise as a top salesman.

That same flexibility came in handy when my career path took an abrupt turn into the entertainment industry. Yet another example of pioneering innovation? The release of *I Am … Sasha Fierce*, Beyoncé's conceptual third solo album. My vision for this double CD was one disc of R&B songs, one disc of pop—something for all of her fans, in other words. As the title suggests, Beyoncé saw it as a collection of personal and introspective ballads (*I Am*) as well as another that contained club bangers in the vein of her diva alter ego (*Sasha Fierce*). Even more foreign to the industry was our simultaneous release of two different lead singles to radio as well as two videos—"If I Were a Boy" for pop stations, "Single Ladies (Put a Ring on It)" for urban formats. At the end of the day, my rationale behind this outside-the-box strategy, which became known as the Beyoncé Plan, was simply music-buyer demographics.

The result? Epic sales. *I Am … Sasha Fierce* debuted on top of the

Billboard 200 albums chart—Beyoncé's third consecutive release to reach the number one spot—and it was the tenth best-selling album of 2008. The momentum extended into 2009 when the album proved to be the second best-selling release of that year.

Actually, the Beyoncé Plan—or the idea at the very core of it—had evolved over the previous five years, beginning with the 2003 soundtrack for her star vehicle, *The Fighting Temptations*, a gospel-themed film costarring Oscar winner Cuba Gooding Jr. We promoted the release as a gospel album even though almost half the songs—seven out of fifteen, to be exact—were pure R&B. At the same time, practically all the recording artists were either R&B stars (The O'Jays, Faith Evans, Angie Stone) or hip-hop talents (Diddy, Missy Elliott, MC Lyte). In the end, the album's sales eclipsed the movie's box office earnings.

A gospel album, you may wonder? Officially, how could it be? Because first I phoned Billboard—the trade magazine that ranks the most popular records across all formats based on radio airplay, sales data, and streaming activity—that's why. "I intend to put eight gospel and seven R&B songs on an upcoming album," I informed my contact at Billboard. "May I still designate it as a gospel album?" Thoughtful silence on the other end of the line. And finally, this response: "Well, no one has ever done that before that I recall—but it makes sense because there are more gospel songs."

That sounds logical. Now consider the out-of-the-box thought process that went into this project. It had to be one of the first times that anyone attempted to break the mold by uniting secular and gospel artists on the same inspirational soundtrack.

In each instance, it was a goal—the desire for a number-one album, plus the hope of maximizing sales to pop fans in addition to R&B lovers—that propelled my thinking to transcend the box. Ironically, the record business, supposedly the most cutting-edge of industries, appears to be a slowly dying example of how boxed-in thinking can literally lead to financial ruin when it fails to keep up with the times and consumer demands.

After all, music is no longer purchased in record stores. Which is why I was among the first talent managers to travel to meet the merchants at Walmart, which is headquartered in Bentonville, Arkansas. How could that be, when it is perhaps the most powerful retailer of media, from CDs and DVDs to video games? Understandably, the record label wanted to control the relationship with such an enormous company and minimize any direct contact with its vast roster of artists and talent-management teams. But Walmart and labels did not exactly make sweet music together. I recall the Walmart folks complaining that they could never get direct answers from any of the labels. Why did that not surprise me? Labels merely acted as middlemen, so each time Walmart sought out specific information or answers, the music reps would "have to get back to you." Then the label rep would need to track down artists and their talent managers before the response could funnel back to Walmart HQ.

I decided to cut out the middleman altogether and establish our own my relationship with Walmart. My guy there was David Porter, vice president and general merchandise manager of entertainment. My relationship with David, who later exited for a major job with Microsoft, explains why we had so much success with the retailer over the years.

Sony could not fully represent our diverse interests anyway. We had multiple products, not just records, to sell through Walmart, including beauty, fashion, even toys—the Baby Jamz toy line, which was inspired by my first grandchild, Solange's son, Juelz. But in developing a relationship with Walmart, I also had to persuade the retailer to stretch its own thinking beyond the usual boundaries. Our first collaboration—a holiday shopping–themed commercial—is a case in point. The idea was to capture the spirit of the season through the scene of a family gathering. True to form, Walmart expected to shoot in a studio.

"No," I protested. "We should film it just like we really do it at home in Houston—with a big Christmas tree, us on the sofa, and a bunch of presents." Walmart initially balked, for no other reason than that an authentic environment was out of the ordinary. "If my family is going to do this commercial, then we are going to keep it real," I insisted. "I realize that this may not be your traditional way of doing things, but …." Walmart ultimately relented and agreed not only with my suggestion regarding the location but also a novel fee arrangement that I had proposed. Instead of writing us a big check, the retailer agreed to stock more than 100,000 units of a soundtrack that we had produced and distributed for the 2005 movie *Roll Bounce.*

It bears repeating that Beyoncé's most recent self-titled album is yet another example of thinking outside the box. I am no longer her manager and therefore cannot take any credit for her latest genius number-one, multiplatinum album, for which she used social media as her marketing platform. I am very proud of Beyoncé and equally proud of Solange for her efforts as a top independent recording artist, singer-songwriter, and now creative director for Puma. Like father, like daughters.

In my opinion, Nike's Jordan brand missed a slam-dunk opportunity in not jumping at a proposal I once made to associate Beyoncé with the juggernaut sneaker. On the other hand, Pepsi eagerly thirsted for an alliance with her. The beverage giant, one of two iconic and rival brands involved in the legendary Cola Wars, happens to be one of the first major brands associated with her solo career. Now she is well established in the galaxy of stars who, by virtue of being allied with one or the other of the dueling soda brands, becomes giant cultural hallmarks in the marketing arena.

Within the army of caretakers who have cultivated this successful collaboration from the beginning, no one stands taller than Danny Socolof. Thanks to his exceptional gift for outside-the-box thinking, Danny occupied a pivotal role in Pepsi's initial approach to wooing Beyoncé. With his consulting company, Marketing Entertainment Group of America (MEGA), Danny thrives at the intersection of music and technology. He studies the science of how each of these powerful variables influences the other in culture and business. He collaborates with premiere brands (Cadillac, Xbox, and Tropicana among them) and artists as diverse as Led Zeppelin and Kanye West.

Danny and I hit it off from the moment we met. Hammering out the Pepsi deal details was tough, but in the end mutual integrity sealed the association. Like me, Danny was seeking to do things that had, in his wise words, "cultural gravitas." We wanted a winning partnership, had a high bar for excellence, and brought the same thinking to the table— talking the talk but also walking the walk, and simultaneously pushing the envelope. That meant I opened myself up to unconventional ways of making classic commercials that enabled Beyoncé to embrace Pepsi in an authentic, credible, and sincere way that was in line with her own image. Danny and I had found common ground—we wanted nothing but outstanding results for both Pepsi and Beyoncé. Since Danny has made a career out of thinking outside the box, he has a lot of smarts to pass along on this seemingly intangible subject.

In my mind, "thinking outside the box" is a broad statement. Certain people work well when given a set of rules, paths to follow, or goals and objectives to meet. They can understand how to achieve success and how their job performance will be measured. Other people thrive when there are few or no rules at all; they exist in a space where they see an end goal. They have a vision or idea about how to get to a place, but no one has prescribed a specific path. They have the latitude—or make the latitude for themselves. I don't necessarily think one style is better than another, just different.

What turns me on in business is to have the opportunity—or to be given a wide berth in a partnership—to create a path to success. I don't work well when there are tight lanes. Still, to be honest, I would not be comfortable having a conversation with myself—and less so with others—about whether I personally think outside of the box. There is a pattern in which I thrive, and I am most happy when given the chance (or I make the opportunity) to be on a path not bound by any conventions. I am most happy out there collaborating with others and breaking new ground.

In my business career, thinking outside the box has mainly been applied to branding and marketing opportunities. But that said, gardeners, politicians, and others in many different fields can also think outside the box, each in his or her own way. I believe that people who are creative generally possess God-given talent. They apply that inspiration and gift in whatever manner works for them. A trait that I have noticed in unconventional thinkers? Many do not fit in "naturally," if you will. So they seek out pastures where they are comfortable in the company of people they trust—people who allow them a chance to express creativity before pouncing.

Unconventional thinkers surround themselves with people who are a bit more forgiving, in other words. I think there is a process to thinking outside the box. Much of my career has been spent trying to peek over the horizon at how music is going to impact technology and vice versa. What does it mean for a brand that successfully latches on to each one of these powerful cultural forces? I explore ways for brands to straddle technology and music credibly— with authenticity—in marketing the brand.

The process involves timing your steps. First, what is your objective? Is the brand that you want to boost a mass brand or a smaller brand? What is the footprint of the audience that you want your brand to reach? Is it mass or early adopter? Do you want to expose your brand to 100 million or 100,000 people? Your filter is this: The unconventional approach to problem solving rests on the size of impact that your brand hopes to achieve. A second step is to think about what I call downside-risk management. The fun part of thinking outside the box is exploring the what-ifs. Granted, considering what can go wrong is not so much fun. But what are the failure points, and have they been thoroughly examined? Where does the whole undertaking potentially come unglued and fall apart? The failure points must be a part of the overall process.

The third, but most important, phase of the process is: do you believe your idea connects with people? No matter what creative people you talk to— singers, writers, marketers, and on and on—they will tell you that a measure of their success is whether they have captured the audience's imagination. It starts with capturing your own imagination. Is your idea thrilling and exciting to you? Come up with the big idea, believe in it, know that it is a big idea, map the target audience, and then count up the failure points. By the way, you don't do this alone. You want to be a strong advocate for your ideas but then have people you trust around to challenge you and play devil's advocate.

In general, thinking outside the box is all about challenging yourself and not resting on your laurels. You should constantly want big challenges in front of you. Don't ever settle and get too comfortable. Don't repeat formulaic approaches. For me, this involves presenting myself with something that is challenging and collaborating with people whose level of creativity is leaps and bounds above mine. That is how I keep my chops sharp.

One fairly recent project, for example, had me working with a client on a mobile payment app. I was charged with helping to bring this new type of behavior—paying merchants through your mobile phone—to the forefront of commerce. It is a gigantic challenge on so many levels that this book would need twice the number of pages to explain. In 2012, another client was the Hard Rock Café. The company engaged me to think about how to magnify the dining chain's social-media profile, leveraging the musical identity of the brand. We designed Global Battle of Bands: Hard Rock Rising. I was able to be the architect of a relationship between Hard Rock and ReverbNation, which describes itself as "the global home base" for almost 3 million artists, labels, managers, and venues to synch up their online marketing services. My description: it's the largest community of indie bands in the world. More than twelve thousand bands participated. In the end, local fans of the bands registered more than a million "likes" for Hard Rock through the Facebook page of their local Hard Rock Café.

Pairing Led Zeppelin with the Cadillac Escalade is easily one of my more memorable examples of thinking outside the box. General Motors was reimagining the Escalade with a bold new lineup and launched it with a marketing campaign featuring the Led Zeppelin hit "Rock and Roll." The effort disrupted the notion that Cadillac was a brand for retirees in Florida and vaulted it back into the mainstream of young adult culture. That was a big out-of-the-box solution that I am very proud of. Another was my role in helping Pepsi establish its early strategic alliances with Apple to usher in a new age of digital music around the iPod and iTunes. In 2003, Pepsi and Apple announced a giveaway of 100 million free songs at the iTunes Music Store.

The most inspiring aspect of my work? Meeting people along the way who I think are the giant creative thinkers of our time. That never gets old.

Outside-the-box thinking doesn't always deliver success. I had the bright—and still stellar, in my opinion—idea to pitch what I thought was a surefire winner. I have no doubt that a kid's sneaker line by Beyoncé under the umbrella of the Jordan brand would have been a swift success. While I did not manage to persuade Nike to come around to my way of thinking, my initiative produced a lasting relationship with Reggie Saunders.

Reggie is director of strategic initiatives for the Jordan brand and one of the most formidable creative minds in consumer products today. Out of the blue, I phoned him at his office around the time that Destiny's Child was reaching the height of its success and Beyoncé was quickly evolving into a brand unto herself.

"Hey, I've got an idea for you," I said to Reggie before proceeding to sell him on my idea. The shoe not only would have boosted the Jordan brand's popularity with kids, but Beyoncé's association would also have brought in women, a consumer group where the brand was not exactly sure-footed. Reggie embraced the suggestion, but the team back at the Nike campus did not follow suit.

Regardless, Reggie and I had bonded through incredible discussions, seeing eye-to-eye on the goals and factors that stars from different arenas can share. In everything we talked about, he focused on the legacy of the Michael Jordan brand uppermost—as I did when it came to Beyoncé.

As a member of the Jordan brain trust, Reggie is perfectly positioned to put his creative-thinking trait through the paces. Sales, retail, brand presentation, celebrity marketing, design, and so forth—the department that Reggie oversees touches every phase of the brand that is recognized the world over by the Jumpman logo. He interacts with the famous product up close and personal while also having responsibility for broadening the brand's market opportunity.

Some people say, "Think outside the box." I say, "Don't have a box, so you can easily see 360 degrees around you." Funny, it's the same premise, really—thinking outside the box and not having a box. Both are about looking for more than one way to reach a goal and not being regimented.

Our brand's DNA is the competitive mystique of Michael Jordan. Every brand initiative must have that in common. We know what we are here to do. We know our storytelling capability. The guy who happens to be the logo is still a human being. So my job is to ask—and to answer—this question: How do we win? How do we empower a winning family? Whether it is empowering our team to be innovative, to take a risk or to take the lead—that's my charge. We have been safe with our brand. Now we are going to branch out and create this halo effect.

At Jordan, we reduce the toughest tasks, initiatives, or goals to their most basic form. Michael refers to this all the time: "Break down the hardest things to their simplest form," he likes to say. That is exactly how we get a creative team going and inspired—by seeking the simplest and most effective way that we can engage with, affect, and influence the consumer.

You have to take risks, but you also need to have a creative vision to focus on. The biggest factor in the equation of creative thinking is trust—in yourself and, if it applies, in the other members of your team. I have been in meetings where ideas are being brainstormed. Someone will react by saying, "That's crazy!" But, you know, crazy can get it done. Who can know everything and not need pieces of the puzzle to help with envisioning the big picture? There have to be metrics for gauging success of the initiatives that we dream up. But trust is that main factor. You've got to have it.

We love our brand—and we covet it too. Our fearless leader, the Jumpman himself, has been incredibly focused. He has been doing his thing for almost thirty years. If you had asked me twenty years ago whether the Jordan brand would be at the level of global reach it has achieved, I would have said, "No way." But Michael had great people—the individual pieces of the puzzle that he developed his giftedness around. And that is how it all came together in the end.

I enjoy sharing the knowledge that I have been fortunate enough to absorb in my improbable foray into the entertainment business. And my love of mentoring young people ranks right up there with my love of basketball. A few years ago, my passions converged through a new acquaintance: Dr. John Rudley, president of Texas Southern University (TSU), located just a few miles from my office in downtown Houston. Dr. Rudley and I bonded over our mutual adoration for hoops—I had played in college, while John was a high school star.

Naturally, as the leader of a prominent educational institution, he also shared with me the commitment to instruct the next generation of success stories. The upshot of this second common bond was an opportunity that I will forever cherish. Dr. Rudley signed off on my hiring as a full-time lecturer in the School of Communications. I cover the gamut of the music business in my course, which is titled "The Recording Industry," including the ABCs of some twenty different departments of a record label—from business affairs, marketing, and artist management to radio promotions, distribution, and creative services. The idea is to bring my students up to speed on a twenty-first century approach to the music business, which began a steep decline at the turn of the century in part because it had remained tradition-bound for decades and refused to change to reflect consumer tastes and demand.

Dr. Rudley, who was appointed president only a year before he hired me, had an equally urgent mandate to modernize Texas Southern. The proud university was in need of an injection of new ideas and energy when he took the reins. Retention and graduation rates were low, as were the university's finances. But today, under Dr. Rudley's cutting-edge leadership, the university has bounced back and continues to flourish.

In our community—by which I mean the African American community—many people do not think in terms of solving problems. Or else they tend to focus on the problem instead of a potential solution to it.

Understandably, people who are down and out simply think in terms of survival. But there is an old adage that has always driven me: necessity is the mother of invention. To me, necessity means there is something that must be done. You have to provide for yourself. You have to be a problem solver. And when I assumed this position at Texas Southern, my goal was to start solving problems on a day-to-day basis, both immediate and long term.

Of course, I had to apply the dynamic of thinking outside the box to my experience at TSU. But then, I believe that all of us should be trying to think outside the box no matter what our job is. In every industry, you have traditionalists who secured their positions by maintaining the status quo. Sometimes, you have to fight with a whole lot of people to make significant changes. People who think outside the box do not have enough company; too few of us want to break with tradition and do some serious risk taking.

Ever since I accepted the appointment as president, this forward-thinking outlook has been our modus operandi in stabilizing and then embarking on the task of modernizing TSU. Our students are clearly talented, but they had not been following the example of talented kids on other campuses. As legend has it, Mark Zuckerberg founded Facebook in his dorm room at Harvard. So thinking outside the box as president of Texas Southern began with a simple question: what can I do to put our students in a position to be as creative as anyone at Harvard or any other college or university, for that matter? Thinking outside the box meant positioning Texas Southern to be known for preparing students for future-economy careers.

Along those lines, in 2009, we introduced an online MBA program, which made Texas Southern one of the first to do so among historically black colleges and universities (HBCUs). That initiative not only differentiated TSU from most HBCUs but also increased our competitive level and paid off financially in a major way. We ended up earning over a million dollars in net revenue.

In a related Internet initiative the following year, we collaborated with media entrepreneur and philanthropist Tom Joyner, the radio host of a nationally syndicated morning show. Tom, a Tuskegee University graduate, is deeply committed to HBCUs. I said, "Tom, why don't you create an Internet portal for HBCUs that have online programs? It would be a convenient one-stop site for people to explore the range of programs offered by all HBCUs."

In no time, Tom started HBCUs Online. TSU joined the Internet portal from the beginning, and it quickly began to reap rewards for us. Not only did we gain top students, but we also brought in more dollars—both of which are critical challenges these days for HBCUs. But Tom couldn't get every other black college to participate. In fact, some HBCUs signed up for rival efforts that were created by white institutions. Along with Florida A&M University, we are still participating in HBCUs Online. However, when we see opportunities to go farther, we seize them, which is what we did in embracing an opportunity from Comcast, the major national cable-TV company.

Again, the year was 2010. Comcast had moved to buy a majority of the NBC television network, related cable channels, and other media companies from GE. As part of the federal approval process for the deal, Comcast had to show that it would operate in a way that served the public interest. That is how our relationship began. And what exactly was the nature of that relationship, you may wonder?

We partnered to introduce the TSU On Demand channel, which allowed Texas Southern the distinction of being the first HBCU to own a cable channel. Best of all, it was free of charge. At the time, as part of the formal announcement, I described the innovative arrangement as an "amazing partnership" that provided "Texas Southern the opportunity to showcase the excellent talent and creativity of our students." I added, "We want to make sure that we shine a light on our students and faculty and that the community sees the quality of students that TSU produces. This is a clear signal that TSU is moving in the right direction, and it gives us another opportunity for TSU to partner with the community and to focus on community issues."

The results that I predicted have indeed come true. Our students are putting up shows and content on the Comcast channel, and it happens to be a great learning vehicle as an added bonus. The kids are getting hands-on, real-world experience—not to mention that it produces some additional income for us too. When we sell ads that run during our televised sports events, we get to keep the revenue. This is the definition of a win-win situation.

Once we got the ball rolling, we began moving along with one innovation after another. Around the same time, we adopted another initiative that stemmed from the fact that TSU is located in Houston, home to one of the nation's busiest ports. The work force there was aging and mostly white. The jobs had become high-tech and computerized. And the security challenge at our port—and, for that matter, at ports nationwide—is huge. Every container has to be checked, and these days it all has to be done with high-tech tools, obviously. I asked myself, where is the opportunity for Texas Southern in those types of circumstances? Not long after, we established new undergraduate degrees in port security, which we announced in October 2010. "These degrees … will be a wonderful opportunity for [our students] to participate in the global economy," I said in commending the Port of Houston Authority for its support, which came in the form of a 2 million dollar contribution. "You are guaranteed a return on your investment."

It goes without saying that as long as I remain president of Texas Southern University, thinking outside the box will continue to steer us forward—and separate us from the rest.

Quiz: Thinking Outside the Box

We have now come to the most successful trait of them all. Thinking outside the box is about integrated thinking rather than a conventional mind-set and approach to problem solving. I believe that the main issues preventing many of us from moving forward in our careers dates back to our early childhood development. To compound the problem, some of us grew up in environments where we looked for positive reinforcement from our parents, teachers, and others, but to no avail.

1. Think back to your own childhood: what passions and hobbies sparked your interest?

2. What are some of the reasons you thought that your passion could not evolve into a future career? Was it, for example, because of your socioeconomic background, your race, your gender, or your sexual identity?

3. When confronted with a problem these days, which answer best describes your typical response?

   a. I believe that there is a corresponding solution to every problem.
   b. There is more than one way to skin a cat.

4. The phrase *boxed-in thinking* applies to people who have been conditioned to believe that problems can only be solved in specific and formulaic ways. Do you consider yourself to be a boxed-in thinker?

5. Take a moment to identify three or four of your closest friends. List their names and alongside each name, identify that individual as a person who either thinks outside the box or is a boxed-in thinker. Now reflect on your answers, which should be quite revealing. Not surprisingly, we tend to associate with people who think just like us.

6. If you identified yourself as the type who thinks outside the box, consider a few instances that exemplify this particular character trait. Write down some of the biggest challenges you have faced—and consequently solved with innovative ideas.

7. How did you utilize out-of-the-box thinking to overcome those particular challenges?

8. How many of the other nine traits of highly successful people did you rely on to achieve a solution?

9. After completing this final chapter, what do you think your next steps to achieving success should be?

10. Of the ten traits discussed in this book, which one happens to be the most challenging for you? I would suggest that you start there.